FROM HORSE TO HELICOPTER

From Horse TO helicopter

John Sutton and John Walker

Leo Cooper · LONDON

First published 1990 by Leo Cooper

Leo Cooper is an independent imprint of the
Octopus Publishing Group, Michelin House,
81 Fulham Road, London SW3 6RB

LONDON   MELBOURNE   AUCKLAND

Copyright © John Sutton and John Walker 1990

ISBN 0-85052-724-4

A CIP catalogue record for this book is available
from the British Library.

Designed by: Brooke Calverley
Photoset in Linotron Bembo by
Rowland Phototypesetting Limited,
Bury St Edmunds, Suffolk
Printed and bound in Great Britain
by Richard Clay Limited, Bungay, Suffolk

Contents

Acknowledgements

The authors gratefully acknowledge all the generous help and advice received from the following organisations and individuals:

The Army Historical Branch MOD
The British Army Review – MOD AT3
The War Office Library
The Logistic Executive, Army, MOD Tpt. 1
RHQ 17/21 Lancers
The Royal Artillery Institution
The Headquarters Library of the Royal Engineers, Chatham
The Guards Museum
The City of London RHQ, The Royal Regiment of Fusiliers
RHQ The Light Infantry
The Duke of Cornwall's Light Infantry, Regimental Museum
The South Wales Borderers and Monmouthshire Regiment, Regimental Museum
RHQ The Royal Irish Rangers
RHQ The Gloucester Regiment
RHQ The Staffordshire Regiment
The Northamptonshire Regiment, Regimental Museum
The Airborne Forces Museum
The Army Air Corps Museum
Army School of Mechanical Transport
Headquarters, The Regular and Territorial Army Training Group, Royal Corps of Transport
RHQ The Royal Corps of Transport
The School of Transportation, RCT
Training and Logistic Development Team RCT
The Royal Corps of Transport, Museum, Library and Archives
Headquarters and Depot RCT TA
Commander Transport 1 (BR) Corps
3 Transport Group RCT
24 Transport and Movements Regiment RCT
29 Regiment RCT
Logistic Support Battalion AMF (L)
Gurkha Transport Regiment
20 Squadron RCT
47 Air Despatch Squadron RCT
62 Transport and Movements Squadron RCT
The Royal Army Veterinary Corps Museum
RAF, Brize Norton
216 Squadron Royal Air Force
The Royal Library, Windsor
The Public Record Office
The British Museum
The British Library – Newspaper Library
The Science Museum
The Imperial War Museum
The Victoria and Albert Museum
The National Maritime Museum – Greenwich
The Royal Naval Museum – Portsmouth
The Royal Naval Submarine Museum – Gosport
The National Army Museum
The Royal Naval Air Force Museum – Hendon
The Blenheim Palace Library
The National Motor Museum and Library – Beaulieu
The London Transport Museum
The Museum of Army Transport – Beverley
The Wellington Museum – Stratfield Saye
The Metropolitan Toronto Library Board
The Maritime Trust
The Ogilby Trust
The Historical Trust – Aldershot
The National Traction Engine Trust
The Automobile Association

ACKNOWLEDGEMENTS

The Cavalry and Guards Club
The Parker Gallery
The Omnibus Society
The Navy News
Soldier Magazine
The Railway Magazine
Knights Photographers – Barnstaple
C. Atlee
Vice-Admiral Sir Patrick Bayly, KBE, CB, DSC
Lieutenant-Colonel I. H. W. Bennett, late RCT
Lieutenant-Colonel B. H. Bignell, late RCT
G. Britton
Peter Brookes
Captain P. J. Brown, RCT
Brigadier B. G. E. Courtis, late RCT
Lieutenant-Colonel M. F. I. Cubitt, MBE, RCT
T. Callaway
David Chandler
Lieutenant-Colonel W. R. H. Charley, JP, DL, late
    Royal Irish Regiment
Major P. N. Chisholm, late WFR
M. E. A. Clease
Major C. W. P. Coan, late RCT
Colonel H. B. Cox, late RCT
Lieutenant-Colonel T. A. Danton-Rees, late RCT
E. Dyas
Major R. B. Edwards, RCT
H. J. Fawcus
T. H. Fitch
Colonel R. C. Gabriel, late RE
W. A. Gibson
Miss F. Gillespie
Lieutenant-Colonel R. F. Grevatt-Ball, RCT
Lieutenant-Colonel H. R. Gulliver MBE
Lieutenant-Colonel Frank Jagger, late RE
The late Colonel R. C. Jeffery, TD, DL, late The
    Northamptonshire Regiment (TA)
E. G. Kedge
Colonel R. N. Harris, MBE, late RCT
Lieutenant-Colonel J. Johnson, late RTR
G. Kilmington
O. F. Lambert, CBE
Major P. Love, late RCT TA
Major L. P. May, WRAC
Miss H. McBurney
Andrew McKay
Captain A. S. McMillan, RAVC

Mrs M. Magnusson
His Grace The Duke of Marlborough, late The Life
    Guards
Major H. F. R. Mason, late RCT
Lieutenant-Colonel D. L. Merrylees, late RCT
Mrs D. J. Bremner-Milne
Major D. K. R. Clifton-Moore, late AAC
Mrs Fiona Montgomery
G. H. M. Nichols
The late Major A. C. E. Notley, ERD, RCT, TA
Major A. N. Notley TD, WRAC, TA
Brigadier P. H. B. O'Meara, CBE, late The
    Lancashire Regiment (PWV)
D. Morrison Paul
Lieutenant-Colonel C. E. Penn, late RCT
Lieutenant-Colonel W. G. Pettifar, MBE, late RRF
L. D. de Pinna
Dick Powell
Major J. A. Robins, late RCT
Miss Pat Rogal
Colonel D. W. Ronald late RCT
Royal Naval Submariners:
    Captain L. W. Napier, DSO, DSC, RN
    Commander A. D. Turvill, RN
    T. Bishop
    N. W. Drury
    R. O'Donnell
    W. R. Pearson, DSM
    J. Scarborough
    R. Ward
David Rushton
Brigadier D. F. Ryan, OBE, late RA
H. G. D. Smith
Major R. P. Smith, late RRW
Major J. R. Spafford, TC, USA
Mrs L. Springate
G. Sutton
Major N. J. Sutton, Gordons
M. D. Tuckfield
Flight-Lieutenant W. I. Towey, RAF
Miss Ward
Major W. H. White, DL, late The Light Infantry
R. Westgate
F. N. Williams
A. Willis
Miss Clare Wright
Lieutenant-Colonel M. H. G. Young, late RCT

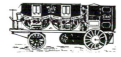

Introduction

FROM THE EARLIEST times armies have used some form of land transport to carry the basic requirements which could not be carried on the marching soldier. These essential items ranged from food, water and spare clothing to reserve ammunition and weapons such as arrows and javelins. *The Bible* relates that David used asses to carry his baggage when visiting Saul. Later, before going out to challenge Goliath, he left it in the place of the waggons with the keeper of the baggage (1 Samuel XVII). Hannibal, too, is still remembered for his classic march from Spain to Northern Italy in September, 218 BC. His 40,000-strong army relied partly on elephants to carry their baggage. For this animal transport he not only had to build special rafts to ferry them across the River Rhone, but lost many crossing the Alps. Similar patterns have been followed down through the ages, with armies dependent on some form of transport for their support. Army Commanders have had to learn to organize their transport, in whatever form it took, and to overcome the problems associated with it. Some have done it better than others.

More than land transport was involved, however, and vessels of many sorts were used by invading armies on seas and rivers to transport themselves and their baggage. Whatever item is required by an army on operations, it will at some stage have to be carried by one form of transport or another, and the provision of suitable transport is thus a vital part of any operation.

The term used for all activities concerned with the administrative support of an army is Logistics. This covers transport for every method of movement including the evacuation of sick and wounded, and everything that will enable a force to take the field of battle totally prepared with all its support for the operation ahead of it. Although a modern military word, and used in much wider contexts nowadays, it will be used in this book ahead of its time. Of this Marlborough and Wellington, two of our earliest generals with an appreciation of logistics, would surely have approved. The production, at the right time, of the right item, in the right quantity, at the right place, is the ultimate test of good logistics. It has not always proved as easy as it sounds, as we shall see!

This then is a book about transport – almost every sort of transport. It traces the many ways in which the British Army has been transported over the centuries, on land, at sea and in the air. It is not about fighting Transport, but Transport essential for fighting. Transport so essential at times, that campaigns have been won because of the contribution that it has made, and lost for lack, misuse, or ignorance of it.

In one book, though, it is not possible to cover in detail the vast and extraordinary heterogeneity of transportation resources used in sustaining the British Army worldwide, for over three centuries. Regretably it is not feasible, either, to trace the complex development processes, many quite remarkable, of every type of vehicle, ship or aircraft employed over the years in the transpor-

Hannibal's Alpine Train, September, 218 BC. These elephants were amongst the many animals that were used to move the army from Spain to Northern Italy. (Drawing by Fiona Montgomery)

children, 'followed the drum'. They helped sustain morale, nursing their husbands and often his comrades, as best they could, despite all their hardships. There were also those women, such as Florence Nightingale, whose intervention and influence were invaluable in improving the transportation facilities for the soldier and his family. From the Crimean War onwards women had an increasingly important official role within the British Army. In the transport role they ultimately became drivers and controllers of military transportation of many sorts. The extent of the problems and achievements of women in families or as individuals, both in being conveyed and in operating the means, deserves wider coverage than this book can possibly give. But, within the book's context, it is hoped that the various examples that have been introduced show due recognition of the importance attached to their role.

Animals, which are so predominant in the story, survived as a vital part of the transportation system for over 300 years, with little change in the way in which they were used. Even when misused, they provided, within their capabilities, an effective, versatile and faithful service under an extraordinary variety of operating conditions. The lack of enthusiasm among many in the Army for discarding them, when eventually the time came, can perhaps be understood.

Today the British Army in both its NATO and National role is transported by land, sea and air using sophisticated, purpose-built equipment, such as the High Mobility Load Carrier, the Landing Ship Logistic, the C130 Hercules aircraft, and the load-carrying helicopter. Nevertheless, the development of the comprehensive means now available for transporting the British Army, both tactically and strategically, has been a slow and sometimes painful process. There have been both triumphs and setbacks. Whenever, over the centuries, the means have failed, it is the fighting soldier who has borne the brunt of failure. The mode of transport for land movement for the first two centuries covered by this book was, naturally, entirely animal-orientated, except when it was possible to supplement or substitute it with river craft. Uncertainty prevailed over much of the transportation system that did exist,

tation role. This volume therefore provides but a glimpse, in words and pictures, of the historical background, and of some of the types of transport involved. Text and pictures are complementary, and where pictures are available to tell the story, we have allowed them to do so with a minimum of text. It is a fact of life, though, that the earlier the period, the less the availability of pictures to illustrate the theme, and so the fuller the text. Overall, only campaigns that best illustrate the theme have been included, and campaign descriptions are of necessity only sufficiently long to present the transportation situation. It is hoped, nevertheless, that the book will enhance the reader's knowledge and provide a greater insight into the part that transportation has played and continues to play in the British Army.

Women as well as men are very much part of this story. They feature both as Army Wives, and latterly as Service Women, in the British Army. From the earliest times soldiers' families formed part of the Army which had to be moved, and such wives as were allowed, many with their

both on land and sea, during this period, and the effort or lack of effort by Government or field commanders to establish and sustain transportation systems under widely differing conditions often put the seal of success or otherwise on a particular campaign.

The ability to move armies swiftly to a chosen place has always been a prerequisite for military success, whether tactically on the battlefield or strategically across both land and sea. This mobility has not been limited just to the positioning of the fighting troops, but also to the movement of all the multifarious supplies necessary to enable them to fight. The means of achieving this movement have had to be adapted to the greatly changing needs of the Army. These needs have been influenced by such factors as the use of more powerful and automatic weapons and the introduction of the tank. The changing tactics and conditions of warfare that have resulted have been reflected in the transportation methods necessary to support them.

The worldwide commitments of the British Army have always necessitated a diversity and flexibility of means of transportation both of the troops and their supplies, but the introduction of essential changes in both the types of transportation and the quantities needed have often been slow and inadequate. Appreciation of the problems of transportation and supply, and the introduction of a suitable system for the prevailing conditions, have proved to be synonymous with great commanders and victory in battle, as this book will attempt to highlight. Improvisation and ingenuity have also played their part in producing transportation systems suitable for supporting a wide range of operations. Many examples of successful achievements inspired by leaders who understood the value of a sound transportation system are to be found. Conversely, also present are examples of failures that can be attributed either to an insufficiency of funding at Government level, thereby not enabling suitable transportation to be provided, or to lack of understanding or effectiveness of those responsible for implementing a system in the field.

During the nineteenth century the inventions of the Industrial Revolution and the advent of the steam engine had only a marginal effect on the transportation of the Army, though a number of officers could foresee the advantages of mechanization and pressed for its implementation. Despite only lukewarm support, experiments in mechanization did start to take place, some instigated by individual officers. It would, though, be many years before the Army ceased to be dependent on animals for its main land transportation. But, from the latter half of the 19th century, as the mix of methods began to include mechanical elements, it was inevitable that at last greater attention should be paid by those in authority to the needs of transportation on a properly organized basis. The resultant changes also helped to reduce the privations which were suffered a great deal of the time by the ordinary soldier. Such innovations as the introduction of specialized transport for casualty evacuation was a considerable advance in this respect.

Until the end of the 19th century the fighting foot soldier mainly moved into battle on land on his own two feet, carrying all his needs for several days. Before then only rarely was he carried in any form of animal-drawn cart, but this was only likely on a very *ad hoc* basis, and some examples of such usage will be found in the book. In essence, though, whatever form of transport was available was needed to carry ammunition, essential equipment and the basic ration of the soldier – bread. As always, there were conflicting requirements for the use of the transport, (if money had been made available to pay for any in the first place) but divided responsibilities for the allocation of what there was led to disputes, inefficiency, and often failure. The cavalry still provided the mobility on the battlefield, but was nevertheless limited in its endurance by the availability of its food and forage, and the transport to carry it. It was not until the First World War that mechanical transport could be used to any extent to provide greater mobility for the infantry soldier.

Organizations in both Government departments and in the field armies affecting transportation were changed frequently right up until the First World War, and it was only then that some semblance of order was achieved. But by then the writing was on the wall. Mechanization was becoming accepted. With it the third dimension was also appearing, and movement of the Army by air was only a few years away. The days of the horse were numbered, but there was still a great deal of mileage to be covered before it could be said, as will be apparent, that the Army had moved from Horse to Helicopter.

Not only has the transportation of the British Army over the years taken many different forms, it has also been operated by a wide variety of organizations and personnel. Many elements, service and civilian, British and Colonial, mercenary and foreign, volunteer and conscript, have contributed to the systems that have evolved over the years. Some can trace their history, or that of their predecessors, back to the earliest days covered by this book, and have been involved with transporting the British Army since that time. The Royal Navy, the Royal Regiment of Artillery, the Corps of Royal Engineers and the Royal Corps of Transport are examples of this connection. The Royal Army Ordnance Corps, the Corps of Royal Electrical and Mechanical Engineers, and the Royal Army Veterinary Corps and their predecessors have also played major roles in the provision and support of transport. It is hoped that this book will provide examples of all those who have contributed. For any that have inadvertently been omitted, one can only plead that a glimpse can regrettably never provide a complete view.

One fact stands out above all else. Whatever form of transportation has been provided, it is ultimately the endurance, resilience and bravery of the soldier which it supports that wins the day. A sound transportation system enables these qualities to prevail.

1

Saddle and Sail

FROM THE BEGINNING of this period of almost 300 years there was the ever-increasing requirement to move the British Army by sea worldwide, to engage in land operations in widely differing situations. It was the start of an era when moving the Army from its home base was to become commonplace in ways that varied from routine reinforcement of colonies to assault landings in enemy-occupied territory, and was to extend until the present day. The wooden sailing ships of this early period, both warships and merchantmen, carried the Army to wherever it was needed, some journeys taking several months. At its destination, the Army had to produce its own transport for land movement and at this time very little would have been carried with the force in the ships. A variety of animals, the horse predominating, provided the carrying or pulling capacity for this land movement, whatever the Army's task. The availability and acquisition of such transportation overseas could, however, be a very haphazard affair, as we shall see later, and involved the use of sutlers, contractors, or just plain speculators, to provide the required means of transport.

On rivers, canals and lakes, small craft of various sorts were used, either because of the necessity to overcome water obstacles, or to supplement the use of land transport for supply or troop carrying. These were also generally obtained locally, if not readily available from Naval sources, and involved similar problems to those of getting animals. As today, one overall problem frequently experienced was lack of money and its effect on obtaining essential resources, and this familiar theme will recur often in these pages.

Although over this lengthy period Naval and transport vessels increased in size, even if not greatly in comfort, and there was some technical improvement in the waggons or equipment towed by animals, it was the organization and control of transportation which was to see the most noticeable change. In particular field commanders were to emerge who had a greater appreciation of what is now known as logistics. Although at first sight their requirements then might be considered to be a great deal less complicated than in modern warfare, they were no less difficult to get right under the prevailing conditions. Success or failure in battle was always influenced by their ability or otherwise to master the administrative problems with which they were faced. This will be seen later to be no less true in the 20th century than it was in the 17th.

The awareness by Oliver Cromwell of the need for a properly organized and constituted Army, even while the Civil War was still in progress, resulted in the formation of the New Model Army in 1645, following the approval of Parliament in December, 1644. With his New Army, Cromwell defeated the King's forces and established himself as a successful and formidable commander. The organization formed within the victorious Parliamentary Army for the control of Transport and Supply, in particular, was to be the basis in the Army for many years to come, but because it existed, it is not to say that it was always properly used. It is not the purpose of this book to examine the course of campaigns, battles, or organizations in detail, but, as the natural starting point for our look at transportation, a short explanation of this new organization is called for.

The New Model Army had specifically established on its Headquarters Staff officers and civilians responsible for transport and supplies. This did not mean that there was a dramatic change in capability on the ground, and as much still depended on the ability of the field commander to obtain and utilize his resources to the best advantage. However, at least the requirement for proper responsibilities was recognized. Although the New Model Army was a far more efficient fighting machine than anything that had gone before it, the split of responsibilities affecting transportation generally, which was to remain right into the 19th century, did bedevil the actual provision of transportation in the field, and *ipso*

facto the maintenance of the Army, on many occasions in the years to come.

On the Headquarters of the Army there was a Waggon-Master-General, a Commissary-General of Victuals, and a Commissary-General of Horse Provisions. The Cavalry had a separate Commissary-General, and the Train (Engineers, Artillery, and an Infantry escort of two battalions) also had special Commissaries: Commissary of Ammunition, and Commissary of Draught Horses. At that time a Commissary was an officer to whom special duties had been allocated. Later the title was applied solely to officers concerned with transport and supplies. In each case, responsibility for what was carried was separated from the means to carry it. All financial responsibilities were placed in the hands of three Treasurers-

Old English Pack Horses. This was the forward link to the fighting troops from the magazines established at ports near to the area of operations, transport by sea being the best way to move large amounts of stores in a secure manner. (National Army Museum)

at-War. Although the basis for controlling a maintenance system for the Army, including the provision of transportation, had now been established, the implementation on the ground was still far from being a reality.

By the end of the Civil War England was almost bankrupt, and although the country was to be at war in one form or another for many years to come, lack of money, and unimaginative control of what there was, was hardly likely to produce the support necessary for any system to be firmly established. Everything was very much hand to mouth, and it was often the mouths that went short.

Although the New Model Army was formed in time to enable the Parliamentarians to defeat the Royalists, little is known of how the new Headquarters organization for transport and supplies actually functioned. Since much of the war was fought parochially, it is unlikely to have been of great significance in the victory. The campaigns in Scotland and Ireland, conducted by General Monk and Cromwell himself, and which overlapped the Civil War, did, though, have to have quite specific maintenance systems to meet the needs of the operational problems that were encountered. The force in each campaign was maintained from magazines set up and supplied from coastal shipping. Distribution to the troops was by means of horse pack transport, which operated with mobile columns. It was these two operations which showed that the new organization could function, but in both cases supply was relatively easy. It was when the Army was involved in campaigns overseas that the system was really tested.

Overall, by 1661, the basis of the future Regular Army had been established, although practically everything for the Army was still on a Regimental system, and the soldier's life was bound up in the Regiment and its organization. The Artillery and Engineers had their own separate organizations. From this time onwards though, evolution would take place within a framework that could accept change more readily.

From the end of the Civil War onwards, apart from combating the attempts by the Stuarts to regain the Throne, the British Army has always had to embark in ships, not only for its 'active service' role, but also for its duties in the maintenance of garrisons in British possessions abroad and defence of what was then a growing Empire. Initially, this responsibility for movement overseas rested with the Navy, though ultimately routine movement was arranged by the Army with direct charter of merchant ships. During this period, though, soldiers were carried in both warships and merchantmen, and even the Naval escorts themselves, when provided, were generally loaded with troops. The largest vessels were only capable of carrying two or three hundred men or the equivalent in horses, and all in great discomfort. Even on relatively short voyages men and animals suffered considerably, and the number of deaths among horses could be devastating. On longer voyages men were quite often unfit to fight effectively when they got to their destination, and it is surprising that they achieved so much when they landed.

King Charles II was on the Throne at the time of the first major movement by sea in the period, January, 1662. This was the occupation of Tangier, a small Portuguese colony handed over to England as part of the marriage settlement of Catherine of Braganza, the Infanta of Portugal, with Charles II. Some 3000 troops and 200 or 300 hundred families were carried in twenty-seven ships. During the period of occupation they were constantly under siege by the Moors, whom they beat in many sallies and skirmishes. However, in October, 1683, largely for financial reasons, Tangier was given up and evacuated by the English garrison. Two ships, the *Welcome* and the *Unity*, were fitted out as hospital ships, the first recorded use, and carried sick soldiers and families, with female nurses to attend to the sick. Conditions on board the hospital ships were, perhaps, better than on the other troopers. For example, the frigates *Woolwich* and *Happy Return*, each of about 600 tons, had been fitted out to carry 200 and 250 troops in addition to the crew. In the event they carried 230 and 330 respectively, and encountered the worst storms of the century on their return journey. Bearing in mind the space taken up on these vessels with the armament, the conditions must have been appalling. The carriage of families on troopships was to be a permanent feature of the

Evacuation of families and sick from Tangier in one of the warships used as a hospital ship, October, 1683. This is the first recorded use of ships converted to this role. (Drawing by Fiona Montgomery)

movement of the Army overseas from now on, though it was to be well into the 19th century before any special provision on troopships for families became a standard feature.

Although the size of ships gradually increased, conditions did not seem to improve, and early in the 18th century these were described by someone who experienced them as 'continual destruction in ye Foretop, ye Pox above board, ye Pleague between Decks, Hell in ye forecastle, and ye Devil at ye Helm'!

1702–1715 Marlborough's Campaigns in Flanders

By the time that William III was on the throne, and his great general the Duke of Marlborough had taken an English army to Europe, there had been little change in the sort of land transport that was available for the subsequent campaigns fought across Holland, France and the German States, as far south as Austria. It was, however, the overall administration and the control of the transport of the Army by Marlborough that was

to have a profound effect on the success of his campaigns.

The basis of Marlborough's transport system was one enormous contract, within which was also incorporated the provision of bread, the soldier's basic ration, and fuel and forage for his whole army. In Flanders this contract was laid with Sir Solomon Medina, a very able man, and it was the waggons that he provided for carrying his supply of bread that were the only source of public transport for the army. However, these 'bread waggons' were certainly not consecrated only to the conveyance of bread, as their designation would seem to imply. A waggon was a waggon and a horse a horse, and they were used for whatever purpose was considered essential at the time. Marlborough would employ either the horses or the waggons or both for the movement of ammunition and guns as well as bread and other stores. Within regiments, sutlers provided the balance of rations needed through regimental contracts, and sutlers had an allowance of transport for their own use. One bread waggon was also allocated to each regiment, out of the general pool, as an ambulance. Roads, apart from the old Roman ones, were few and bad, and, consequently, pack animals were widely used.

The Waggon Master was in an interesting position, being responsible for all waggons and animals once they were on the march, as well as a strange array of regimental baggage including that belonging to the officers. The actual loads carried were not, however, his responsibility. Nevertheless, he had the authority that if any movement took place without his permission the load could be plundered. This included even the Commander-in-Chief's baggage, which was a vast quantity, with ten or more waggons and many pack animals to carry it. Even so, his tasks must have been extremely difficult, having, as he did, to coordinate animals and waggons with a large number of parties interested in their loads. It is difficult to determine the actual numbers of horses used at this stage in the campaign, but later, in 1708, at Lille, some 16,000 horses alone were used for the guns and ammunition. Although some English draught horses were used, most were continental, which were more easily obtainable, and cheaper – a major consideration.

*A 'Marlbrouk' designed by Marlborough and used for
carrying supplies and ammunition and evacuating
casualties, Flanders Campaign, 1702–1715. In this
illustration, carrying supplies from Ostend to the siege
of Lille, note the halberdier keeping the hired driver at
his post. Detail from the Wynendael Tapestry,
Blenheim Palace. (His Grace The Duke of
Marlborough)*

'Towing Guns'. Marlborough's Flanders Campaign 1702–1715. One of the many tasks undertaken by the 'pool' horses. (Royal Artillery Institution)

The finest example of Marlborough's excellent diplomacy, administrative abilities and attention to the most efficient way in which to move his army of 40,000 was its march, in May, 1704, from the Cologne area to the Danube. This was to support the Emperor of Austria and to save Vienna from the threat of a Franco-Bavarian force. The successful movement of the army was to culminate in Marlborough's victory at the Battle of Blenheim in July. The preparations for the march were as complete, and the movement as well controlled, as the strategy of the battle was skilful. Whilst a high standard of discipline was maintained, the wellbeing of the soldier was fully attended to, and everything obtained locally was

paid for. Unusually, there does not seem to have been a shortage of money to pay for the transport and supplies en route, and, with Marlborough's usual thoroughness, credits were arranged in advance with the States through which the army passed. As a result, the army was well received by the local population, which no doubt eased the procurement of the supplies.

In addition to using both waggons and pack transport, Rhine barges were used for conveying heavy artillery and supplies, and all movement was woven into a deception plan to prevent the French knowing the final destination. Marlborough's understanding of how his transport should be best utilized, together with his overall administrative care for his soldiers, provides an excellent model, regrettably not followed by all his successors, as will be seen on many occasions later. We leave Marlborough on a high note, and move on in time, further afield, to an area where the fortunes of the Army were to be very mixed.

The Duke of Cumberland's coach. Used by the Duke during the 1745 rebellion culminating in the defeat of the Young Pretender, Prince Charles Edward, at Culloden on 16 April, 1746. (British Museum)

At William's Name, what Soldier lags behind!
Rouz'd by their Hero, Each outstrips the Wind:
Panting for Battle, to his Coach they hie;
Ride on the Wings, and with the Horses fly.

THE
HIGHLAND CHACE,
or the
PURSUIT OF THE REBELS.
Published according to Act of Parliament 11th Feb. 1745. Price 6d.

If but the Shadow of the Duke appear,
So their known Hills the Rebels skid thro' Fear.
The Eagle, thus, will trembling small Birds scare,
As fierce, He drives them thro' the boundless Air.

1754–1763 Operations in North America – The Seven Years' War

A number of other campaigns took place both in Europe and overseas, principally in the West Indies, after Marlborough's successes in Flanders and on the Danube. However, the next campaign which provides an interesting insight into the operation of transportation under difficult and entirely different conditions to those of Marlborough was in North America. It was during the period after the signing of the Peace of Utrecht in 1714 that the politicians in England had to start getting used to transporting and maintaining the Army in newly acquired overseas possessions. Initially they made a pretty poor job of it, but it is not the purpose of this book to deal with the overall situation of maintenance of these possessions, and North America provides the transportation example that we next require.

After Utrecht England gained Nova Scotia, leaving on the west the French with Quebec, guarding the entrance to the St Lawrence River with access to the Great Lakes. The English with New York had more difficult access to them up the Hudson River. From the Great Lakes there were the important river routes south to the Gulf of Mexico. Clashes in North America between the French, operating from Canada, and the English settlers in the North American colony flared up into a full-scale war when the French drove away some Virginian militia under George Washington. They established Fort Duquesne,

now the modern Pittsburgh, on the Ohio River, to the rear of the English settlements in Pennsylvania. Transportation from New York up to the Great Lakes was normally by river up the Hudson, as boats were easy to come by and maintain, and supply posts were established where there were also gangs of men to carry the boats overland, past the rapids, which barred continuous movement. However, a force sent out from England under General Braddock with orders to drive the French from the posts which they had occupied was to use a land route with disastrous results. This failure does, however, illustrate how lack of a workable transportation and supply plan nullified any chance of success that might otherwise have been possible.

Two regiments were sent out from England and sailed to Hampton Roads, and thence via the River Potomac to Alexandria. A mixed force of those from England and Virginian Militia eventually brought Braddock's force up to some 2200 men. Having selected the worst possible route by which to approach Fort Duquesne, through country where horses, waggons, supplies and forage were scarce and the local colonists unhelpful, the force started with a distinct disadvantage. With extreme difficulty about one hundred and fifty waggons and six hundred pack-horses were assembled and the force set off in

Canoe of the type used for carrying troops on Canadian rivers and lakes, c1755. (Metropolitan Toronto Library Board)

June, 1755, to cover the one hundred and fifty miles to Fort Duquesne. The terrain was such that three hundred axemen had to clear the way for the long train of waggons, packhorses and guns, and even so only 30 miles were covered in the first eight days. Sickness and exhaustion affected both men and animals, without proper supplies and forage, and eventually Braddock pushed on with only half his force, hoping to reach his destination before the French were reinforced. It was not to be, however, and Braddock, and those with him were ambushed and virtually annihilated, Braddock himself being fatally wounded. The logistic irony of this ill-fated expedition is that, even if Braddock had succeeded in taking Fort Duquesne, he had neither the transport nor supplies sufficient to maintain his force and stay there.

There is no indication that Braddock had a fully established organization to run his transport, but clearly there was a Waggon Master of some sort and a Commissary, and the task that faced them within Braddock's plan was appalling. Braddock was a brave soldier, but was not blessed with a great sense of administration, the essential requirement under the prevailing conditions.

It is convenient at this stage to mention two marches which took place in 1763, and again in 1764 after Canada had been won from the French. Both were models of their kind. The Indians had rebelled and threatened the line of posts that had been established to defend the colonists in the west and north, including those between Pennsylvania and the Ohio River. Colonel Bouquet of the 60th Rifles, a very efficient officer, was charged with re-establishing the latter and restoring the confidence of the settlers, who by now were in a state of panic. In 1758 Bouquet had gained experience of moving a force whilst with an expedition under General Forbes. This was the second attempt, three years after Braddock's failure, to expel the French from the Ohio. Even under extreme conditions, it was successful, though costly in lives, and Forbes himself died. Now, five years later, against the Indians, Bouquet drew on this experience, and, in particular, the need to solve the transport and supply problems. He was able to achieve success by careful planning and attention to detail. He kept exact records of the loads that his animal transport carried, very like

modern load tables, and these he subsequently published with a report of the two actions.

We return now to 1758, with William Pitt as Prime Minister in Britain. His aim was to destroy the power of France in North America once and for all by conquering Canada, and to this end the British higher command in North America was completely changed, and the Army hugely reinforced. What followed could be described as a major amphibious operation, but we must limit our interest to the transportation aspects of the two successive actions which formed the whole operation. The first was the capture of Louisburg, followed by that of Quebec, with the aim of exploitation south to Montreal. It took the reinforcements from England, amounting to some eight regular regiments, eleven weeks to reach Halifax in warships and transports. Ultimately, by the end of May, 1758, a force of 157 ships carrying over 11,000 Regulars and about 500 Rangers sailed in to Gabarus Bay, south of Louisburg. The eventual capture of Louisburg was the result of a fine piece of inter-service cooperation and the forerunner of modern successful amphibious operations. But even this success was to be surpassed by that which followed, the seizing of Quebec.

This phase was under the command of Major-General James Wolfe and must be considered as one of the best planned and superbly executed combined operations in history. The fleet carrying Wolfe's force of 9,000 soldiers was commanded by Admiral Charles Saunders and the first task of successfully navigating the currents and shoals of the St Lawrence was in itself a great achievement. The force was initially landed on the Isle of Orleans and it was some weeks before Wolfe decided on his plan for taking what was by now a seemingly impregnable Quebec, built on the natural obstacle of the Heights of Abraham. It was defended by Montcalm, a fine commander, with some 16,000 French and Canadians on and below the Heights. Again, the skilful and effective transportation of the British force to meet Wolfe's plan was vital to the success of the operation.

On the night of 11/12 September, 1759, the Navy ferried the force across the St Lawrence and it made a surprise landing to gain access to the Heights where there was a small path leading up

The landing at Quebec during the night of 11/12 September, 1759. (Metropolitan Toronto Library Board)

the cliffs. In the event, the assaulting troops avoided the footpath which marked the ascent and used every hand and foothold to climb the cliffs. In the meantime, Saunders' naval force had been totally successful with diversionary moves in keeping Montcalm's defenders guessing as to the actual area of landing, thus ensuring concealment of Wolfe's plan. By morning the whole of Wolfe's Force was established at the top of the cliff on the Plain. The subsequent action against Montcalm's defenders only lasted a few minutes, and when it was over, although Wolfe was killed, marked the beginning of the end of French rule in Canada. Wolfe leaves his mark on history as a great soldier, and in the context of this book, as a general who understood the business of transportation and used it supremely well.

1775–1783 The War of American Independence

Although not in chronological order, it is convenient to stay in North America, but this time the campaign which we consider ends in failure,

with the loss of the American Colonies. This unfortunate war, although of significance historically, produced no great impact on transportation history, and the lessons to be learned are those that are by now all too familiar when failure occurs. There is still little change in the types of transportation employed and no sign of any overall co-ordinated land transportation system being introduced. Transport was not yet established as an integral part of the force, and was still found locally to meet anticipated needs. However, these needs were often incorrectly anticipated, and impossible to meet in any case. Even the Navy's superiority on the seas had diminished considerably, and its ability to support the Army at this stage, compared with the successes achieved sixteen years previously, was very limited. To dwell on this campaign too deeply would therefore be unrewarding, but, as always, the lessons are there and certainly deserve mentioning to complete our interest in North America for some years to come.

After the successes of the Seven Years' War both in North America, already considered, and in Europe and India, which are not covered, the conduct of the War of American Independence is in complete contrast, both politically and militarily. The overall military and naval strength of Britain since the Seven Years' War had been sadly reduced, and there was neither the political will nor the military leadership to crush what started as a thinly supported revolt in the North American Colonies. The British Government lived in the vain hope that there were still sufficient numbers loyal to the Crown in the colonies to help preserve them. In the event, as the rebels became stronger, the loyalist numbers dwindled, resources became more difficult to obtain locally, and the war became a logistic nightmare. The combined fleets of France, Spain and Holland, after France had declared war in 1778, ultimately prevented support from the sea, and at that stage the British Navy was powerless to intervene. Without outside logistic support, the British Army in the American colonies, although not suffering a major defeat in battle, was compelled to surrender at Yorktown in 1781.

The course of the campaign, due to the unpreparedness of the British Government, was fraught with the problems of insufficient troops and lack of supplies and land transport. Although a number of raids and skirmishes took place during the early part of 1775, the first major engagement of the war took place at Boston, where the British forces under General Gage, then Commander-in-Chief, were under siege by the rebel army. He was eventually driven to attack a force of Americans, as they were later to be called, who had built defences on Breed Hill on the opposite side of the harbour to the British forces. A force of 2500 under General Howe was ordered to attack the new defences, and successfully crossed the harbour in boats – a minor amphibious success. However, the battle that followed, known as the Battle of Bunker Hill, made it clear that successes against the sort of enemy that the rebels turned out to be could only be achieved at considerable cost in British lives. It was also impossible to follow up this success, since the British forces had no land transport. Once again the force was dependent on obtaining its transport locally, and in

this most hostile of areas it was not possible. Howe, who subsequently replaced Gage, pressed the British Government to send transport from elsewhere, but this proved fruitless. In March, 1776, Howe evacuated Boston by sea and sailed to Halifax, where, in an area with few resources, he gradually built up his forces with reinforcements from England, many of them mercenaries.

The familiar theme that runs through the rest of this campaign is one of success when the British forces got the logistic support that they deserved and failure when they didn't. When boats could be used to convey supplies on the waterways, the problems were eased, but too few horses, once away from the water, meant that supply could not be maintained when communications became tenuous. Attempts made on several occasions throughout the campaign to provide more horses by moving them between areas by sea were disastrous and many perished. Fortunately New York and Pennsylvania, which were occupied by General Howe and his force in 1776, and later Philadelphia in 1777, were able to provide both horse transport and supplies. Regrettably, it did not help to achieve overall success and these were the only areas where success in logistics was achieved.

Logistic failure, and its effect, is typified by the operations of General Burgoyne and his force in 1777. He was ordered to advance from Lake Champlain in the north, via the River Hudson, to New York. Because there was insufficient horse transport to carry his boats and supplies across to the Hudson, and to stock magazines for resupply, he could no longer support his force adequately. Ultimately, surrounded and with half his men casualties, Burgoyne surrendered at Saratoga.

In 1778 the British Government decided to give up the Northern Colonies and to concentrate their efforts on the Southern Colonies, having retained New York. The task of holding these Southern Colonies was entrusted to Lord Cornwallis. There is again no indication of any properly constituted transportation system, and although fighting in a fertile land, most of the supplies appear to have come from the sea with great difficulty. Again, horses sent by sea from the north nearly all perished, but after the capture of Charleston in 1779 many were taken from the rebels. Little seems to have come of their use, however, and the logistic system only staggered along for the rest of the campaign. It was certainly never capable of doing what Cornwallis asked of it, and after his eventual ineffective advance into Virginia, he was pinned down in Yorktown, with any possible chance of supplies by sea denied by the French Fleet. Surrender was inevitable and took place on 19 October, 1781. Although New York was held until the peace was signed in 1783, the Thirteen Colonies had gone.

The ultimate loss of the Colonies can be attributed to the intervention of the French Fleet, but there is little doubt that the transportation and supply systems in both the British, and, it must be said, the American armies also, did little credit to them, and we have to look further afield to find again commanders who were capable of producing a workable transportation system to help them achieve victory.

An East Indiaman troopship at Fort George, Madras, c1800. (Drawing by Fiona Montgomery)

1767–1805 Campaigns in India

We now turn to an area, the Indian subcontinent, where transportation presented very different problems. During the time that the American Colonies were being lost, on the other side of the world the East India Company, which represented British rule in India, had succeeded in removing the power of France from its area. The Indian Empire, firstly under the East India Company, who appointed the Governor-General in Calcutta, and· then, by the end of the century, more directly under the British Government, was being firmly established. This was not achieved, however, without an almost continuous series of campaigns, against French-controlled forces in the first instance, and then after the Treaty of Paris in 1763, against local Indian rulers. We shall only examine these campaigns in sufficient detail to indicate the peculiar transport problems and to introduce a new name to our list of those who understood them – Arthur Wellesley.

The establishment of the British Army in India during the 18th century was to produce a totally new transport requirement, one that was to continue until the British relinquished India in 1947.

There was now a need for a regular shipping service to carry the Army to and from India. The voyage at this time took from six months to a year and the troops were carried in East Indiamen, which were part warship and part merchantman chartered by the East India Company from an organization known as the 'Shipping Interest'. These vessels, which primarily existed for trade with India, were expensively built to a high standard laid down by the East India Company, and were much superior to a man-of-war for trooping. However, that is not to say that they provided much comfort, and the voyage could be very monotonous. They were of about 1200 tons and did have more space for training, recreation and keeping the troops fit than previously provided. Until the introduction of specialized troopships in the mid-19th century these vessels were to provide the vital link with the Indian Empire.

Turning now in general terms to the land transportation of the Army in India, we find two additional load-carrying animals to add to the horse, mule and bullock. These are the camel and the elephant, and, like the others, were to be used by the British Army until after the Second World War in a wide variety of situations. At this stage too, we begin to enter the era of employment of extremely large numbers of animals to meet the particular problems of the terrain and climate, and the increasing size of forces and followers involved. There is another element, though, which was to hinder the effective provision of such transport, and that was the corruption that existed in the administration of the East India Company. This in turn affected the ability of even good generals to pursue, in the most effective manner, the Company's campaigns against the forces of some of the Indian princes.

The main antagonist of the Company's forces at this time was an astute military adventurer named Hyder Ali, who took over and ruled the Kingdom of Mysore and continually harassed the Company. Further north, and spreading right across central India, was the powerful Mahratta Confederacy. By this time it was somewhat disunited, and it was fortunate that mutual enmity and jealousies between all the ruling Mahratta princes prevented them combining in opposition to the Company. Nevertheless, it still took three campaigns and fifty years to curb all their marauding activities.

At this time the Army under British rule in India consisted of three distinct elements which generally operated remarkably well together, normally under the command of an officer of the Regular British Army. Firstly there were the Regular Forces of the Crown serving in India, to protect British territory from foreign interference, and these were transported between Britain and India as required. Then there were the Company's own European Regiments, recruited, paid and organized by the Company; and finally, the Indian Regiments (later to become the Indian Army) recruited locally and with British officers, commissioned into the Company's service, in the senior ranks. As yet there was still no organized military transport or supply system, and provision by contract was still the system employed. Corruption was the order of the day, and extended from members of the Company's Councils, appointed to senior positions in the Army's administrative hierarchy in the field, to the contractors themselves, also appointed by the Councils.

By 1779, after a disastrous failure against the Mahrattas in the Poona area, the British made a disgraceful capitulation known as the Convention of Wargaon. The campaign ending in this misfortune was conducted by a Committee, which courted disaster from the start, and the transport to support it was beset with contractual failures due to corrupt management. This overall setback was followed in 1780 by an invasion of the Madras Presidency by Hyder Ali. Once again, the Army was crippled by the lack of transport and supplies, due to corruption within the Council of Government. The veteran General Sir Eyre Coote was called in to restore the situation, but was severely impeded by lack of transport. The shrewd Hyder Ali had swept up all available transport cattle from the area with his pervasive cavalry, and Coote was forced to restrict his activities to the coastal area where a flotilla of small boats was able to supply him. His Army might well have starved had the French Fleet, which had been in the area, stayed there. By 1781 Coote was eventually able to check Hyder Ali, and saved Madras by three victories at Porto Novo, Pollilur and Sholingarh.

After Coote's victories numerous campaigns were fought against Hyder Ali, and later his son, Tipu Sahib, with varying degrees of success. Success or failure, what is certain is that these campaigns emphasized the total corruption that existed and its effect on the ability of the various commanders to produce the necessary logistic support for the armies involved. In 1786 Lord Cornwallis was sent out to Indian as Governor-General with instructions to purge both the civil and military administration of corruption and to keep in mind the restoration of peace. However, in 1790 he was forced to take action against Tipu Sahib in Mysore. It took two years to achieve success, ending with the storming of Seringapatam on 6 February, 1792. The disasters that befell the Army before this success can only be attributed to complete administrative incompetence, aided and abetted by the success of Tipu Sahib's scorched earth policy. As a result, hundreds of followers died of famine and Cornwallis lost most of the Army's thousands of animals. In order to save both guns and waggons in the retreat that followed, without animals, they had to be dragged by men. It was not

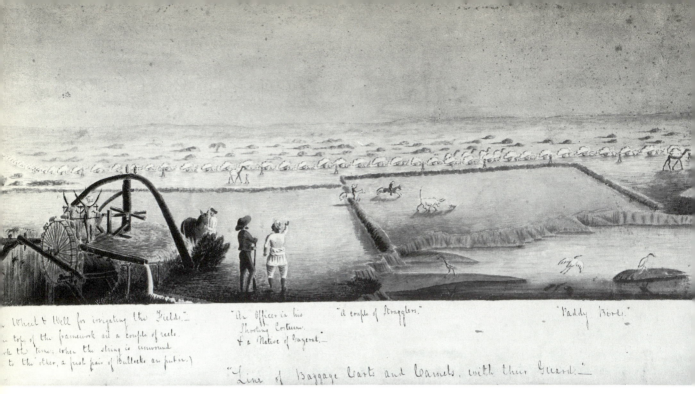

"Wheel & Well for irrigating the Fields."
n top of the framework sit a couple of reels.
k the time, when the string is unwound
to the other, a fresh pair of bullocks are put in.)

"An Officer in his   "a couple of Stragglers."   "Paddy Birds."
Shooting Costume.
& a Native of Guzerat."

"Line of Baggage Carts and Camels, with their Guard."

The Army on the march in India, c1775. (National Army Museum)

until Cornwallis made an administrative plan which was capable of withstanding Tipu Sahib's scorched earth tactics that success was finally achieved.

Before leaving this period in India, one must examine briefly the effect that the 'system' in India had on the then Colonel Arthur Wellesley. He was at that time aged thirty and took part, in 1799, in the final and decisive campaign of the period in Mysore under the Commander-in-Chief. General Harris, Wellesley abhorred the Army's logistic methods and was bitingly critical of them. He subsequently wrote, 'In India, armies take the field with arsenals and magazines which they always carry with them'. His criticism is exemplified by the march of Harris's Army on Seringapatam. The fighting men numbered 31,000, and the followers 150,000. The guns and transport were pulled by local cattle and neither the drivers nor their animals were in any way trained. The force on the move must have been an extraordinary sight, consisting as it did of 120,000 bullocks, together with elephants, camels, horses and asses, moving with the soldiers and followers in a hollow square some three miles wide and seven miles deep. It followed a zigzag course for some 200 miles, with the aim of collecting on the way any animal forage that had not been destroyed by Tipu Sahib. Despite this, the transport

animals soon began to fail, and it was eventually on Wellesley's insistence that the administrative plan was changed, and the transport burden reduced by the destruction of unnecessary baggage. Although success was eventually achieved, the total inefficiency of the 'system' left its mark on Wellesley, and he was to make sure in his future campaigns that his administration was equal to supporting his tactical plan before committing his force.

1793–1805 Wars of the French Revolution

Returning to Europe, we now enter a new era of transport provision for the Army, though, as we shall see, it did not have an auspicious start. In 1793, in continuation of his plan for breaking the power of revolutionary France, the Prime Minister, William Pitt, sent a force to the Low Countries under the command of the Duke of York. This contingent was to be part of an overall army of Austrians, Dutch, Hanoverians and Hessians. As was the practice in Europe, commissariat and transport was arranged through contractors. The British commissary, though, was so late in appearing on the scene, and contracts were so slow in being laid, that the British and Hanoverians were almost starving and could not move for lack of transport. The campaign of 1793 was unsuccessful, but fortunately not disastrous. However, it was quite clear that a new system was required for the transport of guns and supplies, which had been unreliable in the campaign. In 1794 two important new steps were taken to improve the transportation of the Army before a new phase of the campaign started.

Firstly a Corps of Gunner drivers was formed, and this relieved the Commissariat of the difficult task of providing transport for the Artillery, which it had hitherto done. Secondly, a Transport Corps for logistic duties was formed, and designated The Royal Waggoners. Unfortunately, from a recruiting point of view, and for their reputation that followed from this, the latter came into being at quite the wrong time. The Government offered tempting recruiting perks, which resulted in bribery, and a total hotchpotch of manpower being recruited, ranging from schoolboys to ex-convicts. Their performance was no better than their composition, and, although the rest of the Army was little better, they gained an evil reputation. Because they stood out in their blue uniform, they became known as the Newgate Blues.

The campaign, which started well, became impossible when the Austrians withdrew their Army, leaving the British to fend for themselves against a superior enemy. The Duke of York could not defend Holland with his remaining Army and was forced to retreat north through Holland to the line of the River Ems in the depth of an arctic winter. This was calamitous, with discipline disappearing and the losses in men, horses and material reaching colossal proportions. The Royal Waggoners foundered, and a great opportunity to establish a proper transport organization at that time sank with them.

Expedition or Military Fly loaded with infantry, c1798. This is the first example of a vehicle specially designed as a troop carrying vehicle (TCV). (IRCT)

EXPEDITION or MILITARY FLY.
Dedicated to the Hon.ble Association of City & Westminster Horse Volunteers.

An early example of troops moving in transport. A body of Guards en route from London to Portsmouth to embark for Ireland, 10 June, 1798. 1900 rank and file plus officers completed the journey in 10 hours. Watercolour by Rowlandson. (The Cavalry and Guards Club)

1799 **North Holland Expedition**

This campaign is included because, during it, a second, more successful attempt was made to put the land transport of the Army on a proper footing after the disasters of 1794. The resultant rebirth of the Royal Waggon Train was regrettably conceived out of muddle, mismanagement and another campaign failure, but the need for the organization had been established and it was to last a generation before the next change took place.

The British Government had decided that another effort should be made to reduce the power of the French, now established on the Scheldt, and it was hoped that, with the help of Russia, and the possibility of a Dutch uprising,

the French could be driven out of Holland. In August, 1799, 10,000 men under Sir Ralph Abercromby were sent to North Holland, though his orders were vague. He had been provided with a siege train, with little notion of what use it might be put to, but had no horses to move it. Furthermore, the Government made no provision for any other transport. Abercromby protested again and again about the lack of transport for his task and wrote:

> The British troops want the means of conveyance for artillery, sick, baggage and provisions, and you know that we have not a foot of ground until we acquire it. I hope it is not a crime to state these facts.

However, his pleas fell on deaf ears, and his force sailed without transport. Eventually, after a stormy crossing, which delayed the voyage, so that the ships were on the point of running out of food and water, the force landed south of Helder. Fortunately, the French evacuated Helder and so Abercromby had a secure port for his ships, but, because he had no transport, he could not move from this base. After some days a few carts and horses were obtained locally, which helped, but reinforcements of 5,000 men sent from England arrived with only thirty-five bread waggons.

The Government had assumed that, in a country of canals, movement could take place with barges. If the right barges had been available, this might have been correct, but the French had seen to it that those that fitted the local canals had been removed. Abercromby's force managed to survive round the base until further reinforcements arrived, increasing its strength to 50,000. At this stage the Duke of York took over command, and soon afterwards the force deployed against the French. There were then only just over one hundred bread, forage and ambulance waggons immediately available to the force, and about the same quantity were due from England. Even if they had arrived, the allocation was still inadequate for the task. Moreover, the commissary and victualing were in a deplorable state. Largely because of these totally inadequate logistic resources, the Duke was eventually compelled to fall back on Helder, and ultimately the force was withdrawn.

View of GRAVESEND in KENT with TROOPS passing the THAMES to Tilbury Fort

Some good came from this unhappy expedition, as at least it was decided that there should be an established transport organization. But this time the manpower for its drivers was found from cavalry soldiers, and its organizations based upon that of the cavalry – a greatly improved situation. They were placed under the command of the Waggon-Master-General, and, being trained horsemen, they received the higher pay of the cavalry. The formation of the organization was remarkably rapid, but it is probable that at the time less than 25 officers, 275 other ranks and 514 horses served in Holland, about half the planned strength. Not surprisingly the Duke of York, at the end of the campaign, reported that the strength had been inadequate for the task. Inadequate or not, the establishment of organized transport units was a step in the right direction, and the need had now been accepted, at least in Europe. Actually meeting the need in terms of men and transport, would, however, prove to be a continuing problem.

Troops being ferried from Gravesend to Tilbury Fort, c1799. (National Army Museum)

1801 The Egyptian Campaign

We consider briefly the Egyptian Campaign, not from the point of view of land transport, since none was taken by the force sailing from England, but rather to emphasize the effectiveness of the amphibious operation, and the use of water transport for the subsequent operations. It was still not possible at this stage to carry horses in small ships on long and uncertain sea voyages, both from the point of view of injury to the horses, and the sheer size of the problem of providing sufficient water and fodder for the voyage. The question of sending the newly re-formed Royal Waggon Train did not therefore arise. But even keeping a force fed and watered on a long voyage could be difficult, and there was the additional risk in the provision of water from ships for a landing on the shores of Egypt, where in treacherous seas without a harbour, the timing of the actual landing could be uncertain.

The command of the force to retake Egypt from the French, with the aim of returning it to the Ottoman Empire, was given to General Sir Ralph Abercromby, and the amphibious operation was possible because Britain had regained command of the sea in the Mediterranean. Napoleon Bonaparte had departed from Egypt in August, 1799, and the French Army left behind, now under command of Belliard, had resisted all local efforts to remove them, despite the French weariness of Egypt. Abercromby forced his landing at Aboukir, east of Alexandria, on 8 March, 1801, but because of the weather was unable to get supplies ashore for three days. He then advanced on Alexandria, but, since he had no horses, the guns had to be dragged through the sand by his men. Fortunately, he was able to use the salt Lake Maadieh as a means of water transport for some supplies, as, by the time that Alexandria was

taken, a quarter of his force was sick of exhaustion from acting as human transport, Abercromby was mortally wounded in the battle for Alexandria, but his successor was able to find local animals to draw the guns and ammunition waggons, and, using also the Nile for water transport, was able to advance on Cairo, where the French garrison surrendered.

1803–1804 The Mahratta War

We return to India briefly at this stage to consider the part played by Sir Arthur Wellesley as a logistician in this decisive war against the most formidable opponents in India, the Mahrattas. It confirms the reputation of Wellesley as a master of this craft, particularly in his handling of animals used for the transport support of his army. Now a

The British landing at Aboukir, Egypt, 1801. (Leo Cooper Collection)

General, and ruler of Mysore since his part in the capture of Seringapatam in 1799, he had had time for detailed study of the maintenance of his army in the field, as a result of continuous minor operations that took place. After Tipu Sahib's death, the draught bullocks which his army had used, and which Wellesley had observed were better than those of the East India Company, were taken over by the Company. However, despite Wellesley's strong and persistent representations, the Company would not maintain a body of trained drivers. After his victory at the Battle of Assaye, Wellesley wrote to the Government of Bombay, again to make the point about his transportation;

> Money will purchase cattle at any time; but unless men are provided to take care of them, the money is thrown away, and the service must come to a stand. A bullock that goes one day without his regular food loses a part of his strength; if he does not get it on the second day, he may not lose the appearance of being fit for service, but he is entirely unable to work: and after these animals have once lost their strength and condition, so much time elapses before they recover that they become a burden upon the army, and the whole expense of their original purchase, and subsequent food, is lost.
>
> The drivers hired for the service of Bombay are in particular the worst that I have seen (1) because they are entirely unaccustomed to the care of cattle, (2) because of ten of this description of persons hired at Bombay nine of them desert.
>
> There remains but one mode of having bullock-drivers and therefore bullocks when they are required and that is to have in the service at all times a corps of bullock-drivers, regularly trained and managed.

Wellesley was the first General to give any attention to the care of animals in an Indian campaign, and no detail was too small for him in the whole process of logistics. He was still up against the 'system' in India, and the Bombay Government was indecisive and inefficient. However, he was determined that the Army would no longer move in its great box formation previously described, and wrote:

> The only mode by which we can inspire either our allies or our enemies with respect for our operations will be to show them that our armies can move with ease and celerity at all times and in all situations.

To this end, in the campaign with his Army in the West, he followed these principles, and defeated the Mahrattas in five months. Only absolute essentials were allowed to be carried, no hordes of followers were permitted, and officers' baggage, always excessive, was reduced to that which could be carried on pack animals. Above all, though, the transport animals on which so much depended for the Army's mobility and maintenance were properly fed and cared for.

Before leaving India, and following Wellesley to Europe, it is interesting to contrast Wellesley's methods with those of General Lake, who commanded the Army in the North against the Mahrattas. Although a good fighting general, his operations were still inhibited by the old Bengal logistic system of the 'moving box', which, against such an elusive and considerable enemy as the Mahrattas, proved a great handicap. Fortunately, when forced to, he did take action to reduce his logistic encumbrances, and achieved some notable successes. Overall, though, his successes against the Mahrattas, compared with those of Wellesley, were much slower, and punctuated with administrative disasters. The Bengal Government's logistic system was one of overall inefficiency, and whether Wellesley would have been able to improve it, had he been in Bengal rather than Mysore, can be conjectured.

After the Mahratta operations Wellesley returned to the administration of Mysore, where he was very much his own master, and could continue with some of his innovations. In his campaign against the Mahrattas he had changed the face of the existing administrative system to help him achieve operational success. But achieving a long-lasting reorganization at that period in India was beyond even Wellesley. It was enough, and of an inestimable advantage to the British Army, that the lessons that he learned and applied in India he took with him in 1808 to the Iberian Peninsula. It is this time and place which is of considerable moment in the development of the transportation system of the British Army, as we turn next to the Peninsular War.

1808–1814 The Peninsular War

The Iberian Peninsula was a new area for the British Army in strength, previous incursions having been of very limited size. Furthermore, only in the Low Countries had a major conflict involving the British taken place since the sixteenth century. It was therefore very much a new experience for all those participating, and the problems of transportation that were to be encountered throughout the campaign were to have a considerable effect on the progress of operations. The war was long and complex and only those incidents where the transportation aspect was a major factor in the course of events are considered.

The treacherously conceived and executed invasion of Spain and Portugal by France in 1807 was ultimately opposed by a Spanish insurrection in May, 1808. England was asked to help, and Sir Arthur Wellesley was sent with the initial aim of establishing a base at Lisbon, the Portuguese having also risen up against the French. A detachment of 5,000 men, under the Command of General Spencer, which was to be part of Wellesley's force, was located at Gibraltar and was based in copper-bottomed transports ready to go anywhere needed. This was very much the forerunner of a modern mobile force, and they sailed to meet up with the main force off the Lisbon coast. In the meantime Wellesley sailed from Cork with a mixed force of 9,000. It was only with considerable difficulty that he managed to obtain what he saw as an essential requirement of both horses and waggons for his artillery and logistic purposes. In the event, some 500 horses, eighteen gun carriages and a small assortment of waggons were shipped. Since the period of the voyage was uncertain, this was as many animals as it was prudent to take. What was also important was that a contingent of the Royal Waggon Train accompanied the horses in acceptance of Wellesley's demand for a properly constituted transport unit.

At this stage it is opportune to consider the transportation of those wives who were allowed to accompany their husbands on active service. By this time not a great deal had changed in the conditions under which they travelled on ships since this was first mentioned with the evacuation of Tangier in 1683. However, more is known about their overall situation, their role, and how they travelled by land and sea to be able to introduce them more fully into the book, as they accompany Wellesley's Army. Their military role is still an unofficial one, and it is to be another fifty years before women, as well as being wives, become an official element of the Army.

Wives within regiments, with or without children, were selected by ballot, to accompany their husbands on active service. The numbers allowed were six per hundred men, and, despite the privations involved, including even the troopship voyage, the numbers wishing to go were overwhelming. The scenes as regiments left for abroad could be very distressing, as regimental officers, some sympathetic, others not, sorted out the 'to go or not to go wives'. The conditions on the ships, in modern terms, can only be described as appalling. However, they were probably little more terrible than their home life at this time, and were offset by the advantages that the wives saw in being with their husbands. Soldiers, wives and children were all herded together on decks which were too low to stand upright, and where there was no privacy, with only eighteen inches of deck space allowed per person. With little ventilation, and seasickness prevalent, the overall stench on these decks can be imagined. With the voyage from Gravesend to Portugal taking three weeks, all must initially have been thankful to arrive. For many though, the voyage was luxurious compared to the conditions that they were subsequently to meet ashore in less controlled circumstances.

In August, 1808, Wellesley's force, followed by Spencer's from the south, landed over the beaches at Mondego Bay about one hundred miles north of Lisbon, and within ten days everything was ashore. During this time Wellesley himself drew up his detailed logistic plan for the Army. It would seem that his commissariat staff were either incapable of performing this task, or that Wellesley, with justification, did not trust them to do it properly. He then gathered in a variety of transport, including carts and pack mules. This was sufficient to allow him to advance south, keeping to the coast, so that the

Navy could supply him. A complication with the bullock carts that were hired was that their owners would not let them go beyond a point at which replacements could be found, and the composition of the transport support was therefore frequently changing. Wellesley was not, in fact, impressed with the Portuguese bullock carts, as they had fixed axles which made them difficult to turn, and were very noisy. He preferred to use pack mules whenever possible, since they could get off the roads and not block them. However, the total force requirements could not be carried by the available mules, and bullock carts had to be used as well.

After some brief fighting, the Convention of Cintra was signed, and the French were allowed to leave Portugal. The generals, including Wellesley, who were involved in letting the French off the hook, were sent home in disgrace. The winter campaign of 1808–1809 was conducted by General Sir John Moore. His orders were to help the Spanish insurgents drive the French out of Spain, and in October, with his army of some 25,000, he advanced north-east into Spain. In the meantime, a force of 15,000 under General Sir David Baird arrived from England and landed at Coruna to link up with Moore. Baird's force had considerable logistic problems, but Moore's were even worse. He had little money to hire transport or purchase food, and his transport was so short that

what he could carry was below an acceptable limit. He wrote:

> I am advancing without the knowledge of a single magazine being made, or that we may not starve when we arrive.

In the event, he almost did starve, and by December, after a bold drive towards the French communications with France, he was forced to retreat north-west towards Coruna. The weather was ghastly, with rain and snow, and most of his hired transport was lost. The soldiers suffered great privations and the plight of the wives and children who accompanied the Army was frightful. No transport provision was made for them,

and although some wives were able to find donkeys to ride on, others managing to find room on the few baggage waggons, many trudged in misery through the snow, inadequately clad and fed. Sheer exhaustion took its toll, and that so many survived is a great tribute to the resolution and fortitude of the Army wife. Moore, despite all and with great determination, managed to link up with Baird's force, who had been able to establish some magazines on the route. Moore fought off the French successfully at Coruna, but was killed in the battle. Ultimately the whole force was re-embarked at Coruna aboard the British fleet and returned to England.

The entire campaign in the winter of 1808–09 was beset with transportation problems, and even when the Commissariat had succeeded in providing bread or biscuits, or stocking magazines with stores, there was often no transport to carry it forwards or backwards, and stocks had to be destroyed. Moore was entirely dependent on local hired transport, which was insufficient and unreliable, and became impossible when moving over the Portuguese frontier. Although Baird had a small detachment of the Royal Waggon Train with his force, they were to prove ineffective, and were considerably overstretched. Those responsible for logistics in both forces were unskilled and incompetent, and we have to turn to the next phase of the campaign, when Wellesley returns to the scene, to find out how a properly organized logistic system can successfully influence the outcome of a campaign. Even knowing what should be done, though, was not always enough, and Wellesley could only put his transportation on a sound footing when the Government provided the money for him to do so. This, more often than not, proved extremely difficult to obtain.

Wellesley returned to the Peninsula in April, 1809, in command of another Army, and landed at Lisbon, which had been held with the help of a small British force, under command of General Sir John Craddock, after Moore's force had been evacuated. Craddock had tried to obtain, without success, sufficient horses and mules for his cavalry, artillery and transport. Wellesley had no

Baggage waggon with women, Peninsular War, c1809. (National Army Museum)

better luck in finding pack animals when he arrived. His force, therefore, had to depend mainly on local bullock carts for transport, which were too wide for the tracks in many places. In May he marched against the French around Oporto, and drove them northwards. However, he had to abandon the chase as his transport could not keep up with him. He was also burdened with an inexperienced commissariat which he subsequently described as 'bad'.

In July his Army advanced eastwards, joining up with the Spanish. Again he could not get the transport that he required and the Spanish failed to provide either the transport or the supplies that they had promised. On 24 July Wellesley wrote to General Cuesta of the Spanish Army concerning the pursuit of the French Army under Marshall Victor.

> I have not been able to follow the enemy as I would wish, on account of the great deficiency of transport, and owing to my having found it impossible to procure even one mule or cart in Spain.

Although, shortly afterwards, on 28 July, he defeated the French at Talavera, his Army was in a poor state after the battle, half-starved, with horses dying by the hundreds, and with totally inadequate transport to carry the many wounded as well as supplies. It was a great struggle to get safely back to Portugal, and Wellesley, or Viscount Wellington as he now was as a reward for his victory, had learned another lesson. He would not again depend on others for his logistic support.

Those army wives who had accompanied their husbands to war were, understandably, never content to remain at the base, in this case Lisbon, when the Army moved forward. They were determined to travel to the front to be near their husbands, though there was no provision of transport for them to do so. It seems that their persistence at times even caused Wellington concern, as the following order shows:

Badajoz, 1 Oct, 1809

1. The Commander of the forces observes that the women of the Regiments have come up from Lisbon along with the clothing, to the great inconvenience of the Army and to their own detriment, and as they travel on the carts, they delay and render uncertain the arrival of the regimental clothing for the troops, and defeat all the arrangements for bringing it up to the Army.
2. The Commander of the forces desires that Colonel Peacocke will prevent the women from leaving Lisbon with the Regimental baggage, and the officers and non-commissioned officers coming up from Lisbon, in charge of clothing, are desired to prevent the women travelling on the carts.

The Duke of Wellington's General Orders.

Nevertheless, as we know, the wives still found means of joining their husbands, and Colonel Peacocke's task must have been unenviable.

By early 1810 Napoleon had much reinforced his Army in Spain, and Wellington, although greatly outnumbered, was making his plans to defeat it. He still had major logistic problems, with both the supply and transport aspects of the Commissariat, which he intended to put right. We will not dwell on the supply side, although vital for success, but it took all Wellington's skills to convince the Treasury of the need for a proper financial basis for operating the Commissariat, and to produce the money to pay for everything. Our main concern is for the transport system, which was subject to the same Treasury parsimony and total lack of understanding of the need. Wellington battled away to find the money, and made his plans.

He had long considered that, because of the state of the roads and the lack of mobility of the local bullock carts, they should be used to the minimum, and that the Army would basically depend on pack animals for its transport. Only one cart was to be allowed to each regiment for sick. Everything else had to be carried on mule or pack horse, and the allowance laid down for each regiment for regimental baggage was strictly enforced, being some twelve pack mules or horses for the infantry and slightly more for cavalry. Officers had to provide their own mules or horses for their baggage and carts were no longer permitted. Food, forage, stores and reserve ammunition were carried on Commissariat mules; and these amounted to some 9,000 for an army of 53,000. Mules were generally obtained from two sources. Regimental mules were imported from Tangier,

Crossing the River Tagus by rope ferry, Valha, Portugal, 20 May, 1811. (National Army Museum)

and Commissariat mules, with their muleteers, were now successfully hired from the Spanish. However, the muleteers, although well thought of, not being soldiers, could not be kept against their will, and this was eventually to prove a problem.

With his transport and commissariat now far better organized to support his Army, Wellington carried out a series of successful operations against the French, both offensive and defensive, and his logistic system generally stood up well. He was, however, always concerned about the overall discipline of his force, as his soldiers did not treat the local population, on whom he was dependent for many things, as well as he would have wished. There was often plundering when the supply system broke down, and no one knew better than he that sound discipline and good logistics went hand in hand. He eventually achieved both. He knew that to drive the French out of the Peninsula he would have to increase his transport capacity

for a major offensive, and this required the use of more efficient waggons. He therefore had some 800 carts specially designed and built, some locally and some in England. With this transport backing he was able to start his offensive. He still encountered considerable logistic problems, including at one stage the desertion of many of the Spanish muleteers, due to bad man-management. By the end of 1812, however, despite some setbacks, he had liberated two-thirds of Spain, and the Army rested during the winter. In June, 1813, his Army advanced and, by October, had driven the French out of Spain.

The Peninsular War is a landmark in the history of transporting the British Army, not so much because of any technical changes in the types of transport, but in the effect that a much more efficient organization had. New waggons had indeed been developed, but much more important at this stage was the greater discipline that was to be found throughout the Army as a result of getting the logistics right. Soldier-manned transport, though, was still a very small proportion of the whole. Nevertheless, with the proper support that Wellington finally achieved, with a sound transport system, and with the Commissariat geared to his needs, he could indeed say that his Army could go anywhere and do anything, at least in the Peninsula.

1815 The Waterloo Campaign

The Waterloo campaign adds little to the history of military transport, as movement was very limited and the duration short. It has great importance, though, as the end of an era, when much was achieved, and even more thrown away. The vital defeat of Napoleon by the combined Armies of Wellington and Blücher left the British Army the dominant force in Europe. It was unfortunate, though, that all the logistic skills shown by Wellington in the Peninsula in organizing a transportation system, and training the operators to meet his Army's needs, were not accepted as doctrine for the future by the Treasury or War Office. Even for the Waterloo Campaign, coming as it did immediately after the Peninsula War, the Government failed to produce either transport or a Commissariat that was satisfactory. Fortunately, success in battle came quickly, as otherwise the shortcomings could have been as serious as they had been early in the Peninsula.

So we leave this period still without a fully fledged land transport organization. The Waggon Train had been formed, but its establishment, resources and deployment were inadequate, and its ability suspect. Its shortcomings would not be put right quickly, especially with a lack of money which was now to prevail overall.

A private of the Royal Waggon Train entering Hougoumont Farm with ammunition for the 3rd Guards whose stocks were almost exhausted, Waterloo, Belgium, 18 June, 1815. Painting by Charles Stadden. (IRCT)

2

1816–1902

Into the Mechanical Age:
The Changing Face of Transport

WITH THE GREAT victory at Waterloo, the British Army appeared to have reached a high level of achievement both in military skills and in its standing with the British public. This was a deceptive impression, for it soon lost both the capability to fight a continental type war and the esteem of the public. There followed for the Army a period of some forty years in the doldrums. As far as the Nation was concerned, vital peace had been achieved on the continent of Europe, and for most that was all that mattered. The Army's contribution to this peace was conveniently forgotten. But, in fact, the Army, despite the public's fickle attitude, was being called upon to safeguard more and more of the country's overseas possessions and trade. By 1840 there were eighty battalions involved in this task, serving overseas in India and the Colonies, However niggardly the Treasury was in maintaining them, and this it certainly was, they still required extensive shipping facilities to move both personnel and material.

Whilst East Indiamen provided the best troopships to date, there were still insufficient to meet the commitments, and at the turn of the century a number of 900-ton frigates, which were unpopular fighting vessels in the Royal Navy, were converted to troopers. This proved even more unpopular with the Royal Navy crews, who did not like the mundane task of conveying the Army in what were now virtually non-combatant vessels. However, from the Army's point of view they provided a greater degree of comfort than

travelling in ships of the line, and a whole regiment could be accommodated in one ship. Despite this provision of special vessels, ships of the line still had to be used on many occasions, and it was not until the middle of the century that there was any real improvement in the standards of conveyance of the Army by sea.

Though involved continuously in both major and minor campaigns, this did nothing to lessen the disdain that the British public now had for the Army, which they considered an expensive encumbrance and a drain on the Nation's coffers. Infantry battalions, far from the public eye and many months' sailing time from home, were grossly overstretched, and many only survived as viable organizations because of the strength of the Regimental system. But this cut no ice with the Treasury. The purse strings were tightened to such an extent that many of the thousands who died in the inhospitable Colonies were lost because of sheer maladministration by the Government.

It is not surprising that the land transport organization was an early casualty of these economies, since it had never been willingly accepted by the Government as being a necessity for the Army. By 1833 all vestige of a permanent organization – the Royal Waggon Train originated by the Duke of Wellington in the Peninsular War – had been swept away. Just as vital as this loss was the fact that all the lessons on the control and operation of transport so patiently learned and put into operation by Wellington in the Peninsula were quickly forgotten by many of the field commanders, and certainly by the Government. Paradoxically, Wellington, during his long period of power in Whitehall, did little or nothing to help sustain the lessons that he himself had learned and taught. Transport failures were more numerous than successes during the period covered by this chapter.

Despite the Army's situation, and early lack of influence on technical advances, important developments that were taking place in the field of civil engineering began to affect it from early in the period, with little initiative needed on its part. The harnessing of steam to drive transport on sea and land is the first great change in the means of transporting the British Army. The Army took up the contractual use of both steamships and railways as these new modes became available. However, because there was neither the Government will nor the money, and a senior officer corps entrenched in the past, many bumbling and inefficient, the introduction of both technical and organizational advance within the Army itself was to be very slow indeed. As with animal transport in the past, it was still too often left to inspired individual officers to grasp the initiative and fight for operational efficiency. The introduction of the new technology and matching operational organizations was to follow the same pattern.

It took until the middle of the nineteenth century before the Army began to re-establish itself with the public, and this was achieved more because of disasters overcome, rather than from outstanding victories. However, at this time the Army's interest in steam traction, and its possible use for military purposes, was aroused. But it was nearer the end of the century before any real progress was made in the acceptance of technology for more general military transport.

A change of direction in development also occurs in this period. Hitherto development in Service transport, involving techniques, management and control, was largely empirical, and virtually only occurred during campaigns. With entirely new modes of transport beginning to appear, developments that would be of importance to the Army were taking place outside its immediate influence. Interest in this situation

needed to be shown at a higher level, but, at the best, the extent of this was erratic. However, through the century, we do begin to see progress in these developments being made in the home base, as well as the gradual introduction of the new transportation technologies into campaigns.

Each glimpse that we take still reveals the many defects that existed in the operation of the long-suffering animal transport and the various organizations to control it. New technology was equally neglected. There were some successes but many failures. All, though, must be judged against the prevailing political and social conditions of the century, and the varying abilities of commanders to meet the situations with which they were faced and the degree of Government support which they received.

India *1814–1819*

There were two campaigns fought in India during this period, the Nepal War of 1814–1815, and the Pindari War of 1817–1819, against rebels in Central India. Brief mention is made of them because they are illustrative of the numerous campaigns taking place at the time of, and immediately after, Waterloo, and are contrasting in their employment of animal transport. The continuing differences in attitudes and competency in the operation of such transport again emphasizes the lack of any overall system.

In the Nepal campaign the transportation was entirely by elephant and local porters. Movement was mainly on roads constructed by a specially enlisted labour contingent as the force advanced. Only this enabled the elephants to operate. General Ochterlony, commanding the force, although taking operational risks in the difficult terrain, could afford to do so, as his logistic support was carefully planned and executed. He ensured that his means of transportation worked within its limits and was a proper part of his operational plan. He carried the operation to a successful conclusion and the careful organization of his transport played no small part in this achievement.

The Pindari campaign in Central India was, on the other hand, a return to the pre-Wellesley era in

*The attack on the stockades at Pagoda Point on the Rangoon River, Burma by Sir Archibald Campbell, 8 July, 1824. The paddle steamer is the **Diana** purchased into Royal Navy service by Captain Merryatt, RN. (Regimental Headquarters, The Staffordshire Regiment)*

India, and waste and inefficiency prevailed in the operation of the contractual transport. Thousands of draught animals perished from shortage of water and failed logistics in terrain for which this form of transport was unsuitable. The transport system was in total disarray. It took two years to suppress the anarchy, and lack of mobility was a major factor in the failure to achieve an earlier victory. It can only be concluded that all the expertise achieved by Wellesley in the operation of animal transport in India only ten years previously had been forgotten.

The Burmese War *1824–1826*

Apart from the fact that this campaign was fought in a country unknown to the British Army, and little known by the Indian Government who mounted the campaign, its special significance from a transportation point of view was that steam technology was introduced to India for the first time, to carry the British Army in war. This took the form of a single paddle steamer, the *Diana*,

which had been purchased for the Royal Navy.

The reason for the war was to stop the aggressive encroachments by the Burmese on the North-East Frontier of India. It was planned by the Indian Government to use the Irrawaddy River as access to the country, and a fleet, with some 10,000 British and Indian troops embarked, sailed for Rangoon in April, 1824, under the command of Sir Archibald Campbell. Both the operational and logistic planning were faulty, however, and were based on finding land transport and supplies for advancing into the territory once Ragoon was captured. However, although Rangoon was taken with little difficulty on 10 May, 1824, there was neither land transport nor food to be found for a further advance. All had been destroyed or removed. Although some boats of the fleet were available, they were totally inadequate to support the mounting of anything but minor forays a short distance from the river. It took until November before suitable logistic support arrived from India, in the form of boats and bullock transport, and some additional rations. In the meantime the troops had been living on the ships' stale and unbalanced diet. Scurvy, dysentery and fever took their toll. Several thousand died. Even when the British force was able to advance into the interior, they found nothing but complete desolation, and a climate and terrain for which the logistics were totally impracticable.

Another British force was sent into Chittagong in an attempt to invade through the Arakan and link up with the Irrawaddy force. Again, the logistic planning for this force was unworkable and in particular allowed for transport of the wrong sort. The bullocks provided were incapable of operating in the jungle. But it is doubtful whether, even with more suitable pack transport, the venture would have been successful, given the poor overall logistic situation. As it was, few British troops survived the Arakan foray, and from this whole Burma campaign only one in seven returned.

Although the King of Burma eventually accepted the British terms, the force's initial objective of reaching Ava on the Irrawaddy had still not been achieved after almost two years and much loss of life. This was a campaign when the bravery of the soldier was again insufficient to surmount the problems of terrain and climate, when inadequate attention had been paid to the proper provision of transport to support the force with all its requirements.

Outside Developments – Transport Modes

Much of the Army at this time was far away, coping with colonial problems. It was necessarily at this stage based on animal transport for its land movement. At home, very definite progress was being made with steam-driven civilian road and rail transport. By 1821, successful steam carriages were appearing, and the railways were developing their goods traffic potential.

Between 1831 and 1836 steam carriages built by the most successful road coach builder, Walter Hancock, were running between the Bank of England in London, and Stratford, Paddington, Islington and Pentonville. Mechanically, these were apparently very serviceable, and were based on a remarkably efficient boiler. However, it was not until 1858 that traction engine development was considered by the Army.

At sea steam-aided ships were beginning to appear, and, as already mentioned, the first use of one of these for transporting the Army was in the Burma War of 1824. The Army made use of the railways at home from an early stage and the first movement of troops by rail took place in 1830. An agreement was drawn up between the War Office and the Grand Junction Company on 19 June, 1839, known as 'Terms for the conveyance of troops'. However, the Army made use of the railways purely in their role as civilian carriers and there appeared to be no attempt then to build up any railway expertise with the Army itself. This was to come in time for the Crimean War.

The Kaffir War *1834*

This campaign added to the types of transport so far encountered, since it introduced ox waggon transport, the make-up of which was very different to the bullock carts used in India and the Peninsular War.

The commander of the British Forces at Grahamstown in the Cape of Good Hope was Colonel Harry Smith whose plan for the defeat of the invading Kaffirs was based on rapid movement and the capture and removal of their cattle herds. Initially, he looked askance at the ox waggon trains produced for his force's administrative transport by the local Boers, who formed part of his force. These were waggons drawn by upwards of ten oxen and, in the event, with Smith's organizing ability, proved to be both controllable and effective. Although not as fast as he would have liked to keep up with his mobile striking forces, they were never too far behind, and the campaign was won by the mobility which he achieved. This was again the case of a commander who made the best use of his transport, and as a result it assisted him to achieve victory.

The Afghan War 1839–1842

This was a disastrous campaign, which even the great bravery of the British and Indian soldiers could not in the end produce what could be described as a victory. Fortescue, the Army's greatest historian, calls it 'the most insane enterprise undertaken even by an Indian Government'. It was a campaign of enormous overall misplanning and mismanagement, resulting in a great waste of life, both human and animal. The detailed history of this campaign makes sorry reading, and the massacre of the withdrawing Kabul Garrison in 1841, with only one survivor, was a tragic event that typified the nature of the whole enterprise.

The aim of the Indian Government was to invade Afghanistan and place on the throne at Kabul a ruling prince acceptable to the British. It was hoped that this would help to stabilize Afghanistan's position as a buffer state between Russia and India, the latter being subjected to the aggressive tendencies of Russia. To achieve this aim, two forces were to be sent from India, one from Bengal in the east, and one from Bombay Presidency in the south-west. From their starting points at Ferozepore and Karachi respectively, it was planned that they would join up in the area of the Bolan Pass, south of Quetta, and continue together to Kabul.

The operation had all the imbroglios that India had to offer – indecision, wastefulness, political chicanery and jealousies between and within the two forces. There was also total indifference to the maintenance and care of transport animals, and in general a complete lack of realism of what was logistically possible under the prevailing circumstances! Even under the best conditions, the march of the Bengal contingent of approximately 1000 miles would be difficult, more so coming as it did by the least direct route via the Bolan Pass. From the start this deployment presented a considerable transport and maintenance problem. The total strength of the force once they joined up was 21,000 British and Indian troops, to which must be added about 50,000 followers. The route was through appallingly difficult terrain, with climatic extremes of hot and cold and eventually constant opposition from marauding tribesmen.

In the event, with the odds stacked against them, it was beyond the capabilities of those responsible for the logistics either to plan or execute them with any chance of success.

The number of animals that were used on this operation was some 32,500 camels and several thousand horses and bullocks. It is hard to visualize what such numbers looked like on the ground, marching through the passes in a long straggling column, interspersed with the marching troops and followers. The problems of their control and provisioning were enormous, and, in the event, with a shortage of both, the transport was incapable of carrying out its function of maintaining the force against a background of overall logistic failure. During the whole campaign troops and animals were often starving, and, although troops survived these conditions on reduced rations, many died from the effects of heat or total exhaustion, as well as those killed fighting the tribesmen. Animals died by the thousand, or were stolen by tribesmen, because they could not be adequately guarded. 26,700 camels alone were lost. If ever there was a campaign where transport was of paramount importance, but treated as totally expendable, this was it.

The Indian Government was eventually forced to withdraw from Afghanistan, which operation was successfully carried out in November, 1842, when sufficient properly organized transport was provided.

The Crimean War 1854–1856

Victory in this war against Russia can only be said to have been achieved in spite of the appalling unpreparedness, mismanagement and sheer incompetence by most of those involved in the logistics of the operation. These mainly stemmed from faults of the Government at home, rather than the local commanders on the ground, who were faced with often impossible situations, with lack of decision or insufficient support from Whitehall.

It was the first war fought by the British when modern technology made its appearance – in a number of different ways. These were not so much in the confrontation on the battlefield as in

all the other facets of war. Steamships, providing more rapid transport from the home base (though not always used to the best advantage in provisioning the force), were firmly established. Railways too were by now widespread in Britain and were used for troop movement to the ports. They also provided the means of a more rapid conveyance of news of the war to the general public, by the faster and wider distribution of newspapers. The telegraph was also available, not only for military despatches, but for newspaper correspondents as well, and this, then as now, led to conflict on what should or should not be published about the operations! Newspaper reports were, however, to lead to more public awareness of the general state in which the Army was having to live and operate. As a result, reforms in step with those then occurring in civil life were to take place to improve the general welfare of the soldier, and ultimately the overall efficiency of the Army, including its transportation.

We are now, however, concerned with the immediate transport matters in the campaign area. Transportation in this campaign had expanded as a result of the introduction of railways. Nevertheless they were still only to play a small part, as the force was still dependent on animal transport for the bulk of its land movement. At this stage the major change in land transport was in management and control. There were also some improvements in animal-drawn vehicles. Better ambulances, specially designed, were part of the transformation of the hospital services, under the guidance of Florence Nightingale. It was also the last campaign in which wives were chosen by ballot to accompany their husbands on active service and were allowed to travel to war with them on a troopship. There were, however,

more important implications for wives travelling on troopships as a result of this campaign, since steps were taken after it greatly to improve both the number of families allowed to travel to overseas stations and the conditions under which they travelled.

We need not dwell on the reasons for this war, into which the Government drifted with the French and Turks as allies. At the start of the campaign, because of Government policies, there was virtually no administrative staff or services left in the Army. The Commissariat, responsible for supply in the field, had been done away with, and there was no land transport organization responsible for carrying the supplies that it should have provided. The force therefore, from a logistic point of view, started with distinct disadvantages for a continental war of this sort, the Army having got by with very little in colonial campaigns over the past thirty years.

The British Army element, under Lord Raglan, numbered some 26,000 and were sent to Gallipoli or Scutari, via Malta. The Commissariat, still a civilian organization, was hastily reformed under a Commissary General, the elderly and rather difficult Mr William Filder. He was a veteran of the Peninsular War and was responsible, in the theatre, for the logistics for the force, including all the sea and land transport. The organization, though, was greatly hampered by bureaucratic direction from London. Despite Filder's personal efforts, he could not work miracles, and a major operation of this nature required a fully trained organization. The chaotic results more than proved that it did not exist. Eventually, despite Filder's misgivings on the logistic situation, all the force was transferred to Varna. In the meantime, Raglan had realized the necessity for a proper transport organization, and, in June, 1854, asked the Government to form and send out a land transport corps. By then, it had been decided, against the judgement of the field commanders, to move the force from Varna to Balaclava, and to lay siege to the main Russian port of Sevastopol.

The movement to Balaclava of 33,452 men and 3,349 horses was carried out by 24 steam transports, 64 sailing transports, four commissioned screw steamers and 1 commissioned sailing ship.

*The sinking of the **Birkenhead** at Point Danger, South Africa on 27 February, 1852. Originally built at Birkenhead in 1846 as a steam frigate fitted with paddles, it was later converted into a transport. It was one of the first steel-hulled ships and was later discarded by the Admiralty as steel was considered to be too heavy. Of the 680 on board, 193, including all the women and children, were saved. Their safety was assured by the steadfastness of the troops who remained on parade until the ship broke up. (The Parker Gallery)*

GOING TO THE WAR.

EMBARKATION OF THE 93rd HIGHLANDERS AT PLYMOUTH, MARCH 16, 1854, IN THE GREAT STEAM SHIP HIMALAYA.

An important landmark in the history of trooping was the presence in the fleet of the Peninsular and Oriental Steam Navigation Company's steamship *Himalaya* as a trooper for this campaign. This 3,438-ton vessel was then the largest steamship afloat, but had proved uneconomical for P & O. They were happy to be relieved of their financial burden, with her purchase by the Government as a trooper, in which capacity she proved ideal. The Government also chartered eleven other P & O ships for the campaign, which carried some 62,000 officers and men and 15,000 horses overall. These steamships provided reasonable comfort for the soldiers, but the conditions on the sailing ships were frequently very bad, soldiers often having to travel as deck passengers in the middle of winter.

The tiny harbour of Balaclava, which was the only port, was crammed with shipping. Apart from anything else, this was ultimately a health hazard. The main problem associated with it, however, was the means of inland communication. It was some eight miles from the British camp established south of Sevastopol and there was no direct road from the harbour to the camp. The lack of a suitable road was later to prove a tremendous liability to the force.

Embarkation of the 93rd Highlanders, now the Argyll and Sutherland Highlanders (Princess Louise's), at Plymouth on 1 March, 1854 in the steamship **Himalaya**. *The ship was built for the Pacific and Orient Line just before the Crimean War. Of 3,438 tons, the ship could steam at fourteen knots and sixteen and a half knots sail-assisted. Finally sunk by German bombers in Portland Harbour, Dorset, in 1942 where she was being used as a hulk. (National Army Museum)*

The winter of 1854 was spent by most of the force on the plains overlooking Sevastopol. The weather and living conditions were appalling, and there was little transport to take supplies of every sort from the harbour to the camp, since there was no forage on which to feed the transport animals. Sickness threatened to exterminate the Army and a disastrous storm destroyed the camp and many ships carrying supplies. The road being built from the harbour to the camp was a sea of mud and almost impassable. Government support was intolerable and vital stores took many months to reach the area of operations, despite the speed at which it could now be transported in steam ships. Eventually, a now-informed British public realized the situation, and in January, 1855, the Government fell, to be replaced by one committed to improving the situation in the Crimea. Two major transportation events then took place. A labour force was sent out from England to build a railway from the harbour to the camp and a Land Transport Corps was formed.

The railway, initially operated by a civilian organization, was eventually taken over by the Army, who were to increase greatly the quantity of stores moved, from 400 to 700 tons a day. Sick and wounded were evacuated from the camp to the harbour in the trucks which had taken up the stores, the first time that the British Army used a railway for the evacuation of casualties.

The Land Transport Corps was formed in some haste and there were many flaws in its composition and operating ability as a result. The new Corps was placed under the auspices of the

War Office instead of the Treasury, who had previously controlled transport, and was a military organization. The Commissariat, which had previously controlled transport in the field, remained civilian-manned. Regrettably, neither the officers nor the men selected were of the right calibre, as the terms of service had been completely misjudged, and standards were very low. Although the frightful winter of 1854 was behind them, by the end of 1855 the Land Transport Corps had failed to come up to expectations and

RIGHT *The Commissariat difficulties. The road from Balaclava to Sevastopol at Kadikoi during wet weather, Crimea, 1854. (National Army Museum)*

LEFT *Progress of the Balaclava railway to Kadikoi, March, 1855. (School of Transportation, RCT)*

was in danger of breaking down. It was then completely reorganized and by 1856 was at last providing the effective organization so long overdue. It is interesting to speculate how many of the logistic failures of 1854 might have been prevented if a proper transport organization had been available from the start.

Florence Nightingale, whose work for the sick and wounded at Scutari hospital and her influence on the future of nursing is well known, is not generally associated with transportation. Satisfactory conveyance of the sick and wounded is a prerequisite to saving lives and was something that concerned her greatly. When 70,000 soldiers died from sickness alone in the Crimea, and most could not be transported for satisfactory treatment, her concern was certainly not misplaced. She had started action on the transport problems when arriving at Scutari in November, 1854. She asked the British Ambassador to Turkey for twelve horse-drawn vehicles to convey the wounded from the beach to the hospital at Scutari, but he was un-cooperative. His wife, however, provided seven gilt and glass coaches and five other vehicles, which Florence Nightingale paid for out of her own pocket! She continued to have many battles with local officials over the transportation of the wounded. Her influence not only extended to ambulances, but also to hospital ships, and there were ultimately many improvements overall as a result of her work.

In 1856, at the end of the campaign, the Land Transport Corps was renamed the Military Train. In 1858, despite the protestations of Sir William Codrington, who had been Commander-in-Chief after the fall of Sevastopol, it was reduced to a mere 1100 men. As a result, it was not ready when next required and took time to re-establish.

BELOW *Doctor Smith's new hospital waggon at the siege of Sevastopol (National Army Museum)*

TOP RIGHT *Miss Nightingale's carriage. (National Army Museum)*

BOTTOM RIGHT *The Hospital Department and Surgery, HMS **Melbourne**, 1855. (RN Museum, Portsmouth)*

SIEGE OF SEBASTOPOL—DR. SMITH'S NEW HOSPITAL WAGGONS.

MISS NIGHTINGALE'S CARRIAGE AT THE SEAT OF WAR.—(SEE NEXT PAGE.)

THE HOSPITAL DEPARTMENT AND SURGERY.

The Indian Mutiny *1857–1858*

Although many events in the Indian Mutiny are of overall historical interest, they are well chronicled elsewhere and transportation matters will be touched on only briefly, since they largely display little more skill in the handling of these matters than in the immediate post-Wellesley campaigns in India. There are nevertheless some transportation aspects which are significant. At the time of the Mutiny little had changed in the transport system operating within the Army in India, but civil railway development had started in various parts of India, though understandably well behind that in Britain, as the distances were enormous. The Indian Government was just as dilatory as in the past in assisting its field commanders in providing adequate logistics for operations, and again, very much depended on the ability of individual commanders, and whether or not they could utilize the available resources to the best advantage.

When the uprising started in Meerut in May, 1857, the European element of the Army in India consisted of five cavalry regiments and twenty-nine infantry battalions of the combined Imperial and East India Company regiments. Seven battalions were serving outside India in areas of Indian Government responsibility. Those in India were spread very thinly, with twelve still in the Punjab after the recent Sikh War. Distances from these locations to the centres of the mutiny at Delhi, Lucknow and Cawnpore were great. Transport was essential for concentrating any force, but all the military transport organizations had been disbanded on financial grounds. Movement was, as before, dependent on obtaining transport from local contractual resources. This was now an uncertain business, since the bazaars were seething with rumour and contractors were apprehensive of the effect on their future of continuing to co-operate with the British. Gathering transport was therefore a more lengthy process and relief columns were held up until animals and vehicles were found. Some troop movement by railway was possible and did take place several

Troops on the march. Indian Mutiny, 1857. (National Army Museum)

times throughout the period, but the bulk of the lines then in existence did not help the movement of troops from or to the right places.

General Havelock, with a small column, delayed by lack of transport, was unable to relieve the Cawnpore Garrison until all in it had been massacred. Subsequently, in September, his reinforced column successfully reached and defeated the rebels laying siege to the Lucknow Garrison, but could not then evacuate the occupants because the additional transport required was unobtainable. The Garrison was eventually relieved in November by a column under the command of Sir Colin Campbell, who by that time had gathered adequate transport and supplies. He had indeed found sufficient to enable him for the rest of the operations to resort to the old Indian practice of travelling with an enormous collection of impedimenta and followers. Had the mutineers been more strategically competent, they could have caused him some difficulty, since real mobility had again been discarded.

There was, however, during the operations, some indication of a greater awareness of the advantages of road transport to carry the infantry, thus providing more mobility and lessening their fatigue prior to engaging the enemy. General Neil mounted some of his force from the Royal Dublin Fusiliers, known as Neil's Blue Caps, in such transport. Although experiments had taken place in England just before 1800, little use was subsequently made of troop-carrying transport, and it was to be many years before the infantry were carried into battle in any numbers by road. The General was also involved in rail movement, and had occasion to have the Stationmaster at Calcutta station arrested for refusing to hold a train to move his troops. The railway line at that time extended from Calcutta to Moniganj, a distance of about 120 miles.

The final transportation interest in this campaign is centred round the operations of General Sir Hugh Rose in January, 1858. These involved a march of 1,000 miles across Central India, from Mhow to Kalpi on the River Jumna. He had planned his transport most carefully and practiced the Wellesley art of cutting out all non-essentials and looking after his animals, mostly camels. By this time, also, a detachment of the Military Train

had arrived from England and joined his force. Unfortunately, as transport operators they were not to prove effective. Their officer and soldier recruitment was unsatisfactory, as had been that of their predecessors, the Land Transport Corps, only two years previously. They were too cavalry-minded and tended to look down on working with the Commissariat, who were still civilianized. They performed bravely and successfully enough when operating as cavalry, which they were given opportunities to do, but this was not their primary role, and in that they failed. Reporting on their lack of effectiveness in their transport role, Sir Hugh Rose, who was perhaps the most able commander in India during the Mutiny, complained of disorganized and inefficient transport all the way from Bombay to the Jumna.

Yet another attempt to produce a well-found, established transport organization had failed, and the suppression of the mutineers had left the British Army, certainly in India, no further forward in this respect. Regrettably, there was to be no improvement in this situation by the time that the next campaign, fought in China, was over.

The China War 1860

Although only a small campaign, it is included because it demonstrates that the now established transport service was still in disarray. This applied just as much in India during the Mutiny, where the Army was already established, as when it was part of a force for an externally mounted campaign, such as the Crimean War. In China the force, which came mainly from India, assembled in Hong Kong. A battalion of the Military Train was sent out from England and was made responsible both for obtaining transport animals from around the Far East and for the operation of all the land transport. A great mixture of animals was eventually collected – horses, asses, pack mules and bullocks, some 2500 in all, with 2000 civilian drivers, for whom the Military Train provided supervision. In addition about 3000 Chinese porters were employed. In the event, it was lack of adequate supervision that proved the major failing. From the start the element of the

The Commander Royal Engineers (CRE) and Deputy Assistant Adjutant General (DAAG) en route to call on Government House. The China Campaign, 1857. (National Army Museum)

Military Train responsible for organizing this, admittedly, motley collection, was singularly unsuccessful in producing effective, working transport support. However, the force of some 14,000 British, and their French allies, who produced their own logistic backing, sailed in May, 1860, in a fleet of about 200 vessels to the Gulf of Pechili, to land on mainland China.

After some delays while stores were gathered and transport sorted out, on 21 August the force successfully captured their first objective, the Taku Forts. This was a notable achievement and they were then able to go on to occupy Tientsin. Here, while diplomatic negotiations were taking place with the Chinese, many of the transport animals and their drivers disappeared – spirited away by the wily Chinese. There was, therefore, a delay before the force could continue its advance on Pekin which, notwithstanding the delay, surrendered on 13 October.

It could be said, once again, that the campaign was successful in spite of logistic failings, though it is true that this time it resulted in delays in the operation, rather than being the cause of any suffering to the troops. The disagreement which had started in the Crimea between the Commissariat and the Land Transport Corps continued with greater ferocity between the Commissariat and the Military Train in China. There were faults on both sides, but it is worth reiterating the main problems involved. Transport had ceased to be a responsibility of the Commissariat, but the Military Train regarded the Commissariat as inferior beings and themselves as 'semi-dragoons', too superior to get down to the real business of transport management – their *raison d'être*. On the other hand the Commissariat still considered that they should control all transport. They had the material to be carried and considered that the

Military Train should transport it under their orders. Had the Military Train been composed of the right sort of personnel, with the training, skills and enthusiasm to carry out their new role, the differences might have been resolved. As it was, the Military Train was blamed for many of the overall shortcomings of the logistic system.

The main premise put forward by a number of eminent senior officers reporting on the logistic problems of the China War was that one organization should control both the provision of food and its transportation. The Commissariat was still considered by most to be the best organization for this task. It still suffered, though, in the eyes of many from being a civilian organization, whereas the Military Train was composed of military personnel, albeit, at this time, badly recruited. Combining the two organizations again was not to occur for twenty-eight years, when the Army Service Corps was formed as a completely military body.

A soldier of the Military Train escorting the Chinese Coolie Corps, wheelbarrow and supporters during the China Campaign, 1860. (Drawing by Fiona Montgomery)

Transportation and Systems Development *Mid 19th Century*

While campaigns were being fought all over the world, displaying a few advances in technology but rather less in organization, control and operation of transport, there were more signs of advancement off the battlefield. This section considers what these were at that time.

By 1850 the steam traction engine was being developed for agricultural use. This created some military interest, and the Royal Artillery at Woolwich saw its potential. In 1858 an 8-ton Bray steam tractor was used to haul 68-pounder guns, which it did at an average speed of 2.3 mph. There were problems, however, over the damage to road surfaces caused by these vehicles. Although various devices were tried, including one known as the Tuxford Boydell Endless Railway, which enabled wheels to grip without tearing up the road, the general restrictions on the civilian use of steam engines on roads held back more rapid development. Steam tractors continued to be used mainly for agriculture. However, the Royal Engineers saw a more general service use for this type of transport, when a much lighter machine produced by Aveling and Porter in 1868 became available. This weighed 16¾ tons and was used for a variety of Royal Engineer tasks. It, and future developments up until 1894, were known as 'Steam Sappers'. In 1899 the 'Traction Engines', as the name was changed to in 1894, went to the Boer War and their operations there are dealt with under that campaign.

In 1868 Lieutenant R. E. B. Crompton of the Rifle Brigade was the first soldier to develop a mechanical vehicle. This officer was destined to become a leading figure in the field of civil electrical engineering, as well as a pioneer in the use of steam traction engines in the Army. He later played a leading part in the conversion of the Army from the steam engine to the internal combustion engine. He started his pioneering efforts in India, when he was only 26 and newly married, and we give a very brief outline of his early contribution to Army transport, which, during his lifetime, was enormous. This astonishing man lived until he was 95.

While still at Harrow School he built a steam

traction engine named Bluebelle, which he subsequently shipped out to India and used to tour on his honeymoon. In 1868 he persuaded the Viceroy, Lord Mayo, that steam traction engines had a future in road transport and successfully demonstrated their effectiveness. In conjunction with R. W. Thomson, who developed the solid rubber tyre and so overcame the road damage problem, Crompton produced four road trains for use in India. These were employed for regular goods and passenger traffic between 1873 and 1878. In 1873, three engines, the Chenab, the Ravee and the Indus, took part in military manoeuvres. They proved their ability, demonstrating the far greater loads that they could move compared with the animal transport. The manoeuvres were witnessed by General Lord Roberts, which was to have important implications when the Boer War started some years later.

TOP *Boydell's Endless Railway, 1857. The flat plates attached to a hinge at the periphery of the wheel forming, in effect, a self-laying platform increasing cross-country performance and reducing damage to existing roads. (IRCT)*
BOTTOM *Lieutenant R. E. B. Crompton, Rifle Brigade, built his first mechanical vehicle whilst still at school and shipped it out to India in 1868. (IRCT)*
MAIN PICTURE *Although the Army was generally taking little interest in steam road transport, some development was taking place. This six nominal horse-power Steam Sapper built by Aveling and Porter of Rochester, Kent and train, loaded with siege stores, was photographed outside the School of Military Engineering, Chatham, Kent in 1877. (IRCT)*

Crompton established the fact that, with his transport system, both for the military transport of troops and stores as well as for commercial use, loads on suitable surfaces could be carried at three times the speed of animal transport. The cost per ton mile was also less than half the cost of animal transport, even allowing for tyre wear costs, which were gradually improving as techniques advanced. Crompton returned to England in 1875 to find that the railways had monopolized interest and money, and both in Britain and India development of mechanized road transport was shelved. He left the Army in 1876 and, finding that there was no interest in road transport, turned to electrical engineering. He was to establish a very considerable reputation in this field. He fortunately returned to the Army in 1899, having established, on his own initiative, a volunteer force of electrical engineers, and, at Lord Roberts' instigation, once again applied his skills to Army transport. We shall follow Crompton's activities at this time in the Boer War section.

While technical developments in Army road transport slowly took place, some progress, too, was being made in the establishment of a permanent transport organization. It is impossible to deal with this in anything but a brief outline, as the complex political and military ramifications were spread over a long period and were often acrimonious, ill-founded and confusing for all.

In 1855 the transfer of responsibility for the Commissariat and Transport from the Treasury to the War Office, although a good thing in the long run, had caused great confusion in its implementation. This has been touched on earlier. No one involved liked the organization that had sprung up. It was split into an unsatisfactory militarized transport organization, under various titles and guises, and a civilian commissariat, smarting from the loss of control that it previously had over the transport that carried its supplies. But at least Parliament now recognized that the Army needed permanent transport. Dealing with it was a different matter, however. Among the numerous committees appointed at the time to deal with the overall situation in the Army was one under Lord Strathnairn in 1866, to consider the organization of supplies and transport. As a result of the deliberations of this Committee, the

Army went through a series of reorganizations for the control and operation of supplies and transport, with various political and military permutations for combining the roles. The totally confusing changes that resulted were not settled until 1888, when the Army Service Corps was established. The effect that these changes had will be considered in the campaigns dealt with in the remainder of this chapter.

The Abyssinian Expedition 1867

This successful campaign, at the request of the Imperial Government, was mounted from India. Theodore, an Abyssinian noble, had, in 1855, declared himself King of Ethiopia. Though unentitled, no one was in a position to deny him. He was friendly at first to Europeans, but power went to his head and he not only became a tyrant in his own land, but took captive a number of British officials, other Europeans and families which he held at Magdala, his capital. Despite protests from the British Government, he declined to release them and the aim of the campaign was to unseat Theodore and release the captives.

Apart from the very considerable difficulties of the operational task, producing the necessary logistic backing presented formidable problems. Despite an inauspicious start, fortunately not catastrophic, this backing eventually gave the determined and resolute force the resources that it needed to succeed.

The transportation facilities were a mixture of the new technology – a purpose-built railway, better hospital ships, modern shipping providing drinking water (in very short supply from local sources) from condensers – and the old Indian practice of hired drivers for the animal transport, with lack of overall control and management.

Magdala was over 400 miles from the nearest suitable landing area on the Red Sea and to reach it involved crossing some twelve miles of semi-desert, ascending 7,000 feet through fifty miles of passes, and then an approach march of 350 miles to Magdala, a fortress stronghold standing at 10,000 feet. The climate ranged from the extremes of very high temperatures on the coast to very cold nights in the highlands.

The force of 12,600 British and Indian troops, with 14,500 followers, was commanded by General Sir Robert Napier, who had no doubts about the logistic problems involved. He tried from the start to establish a proper transport organization with military officers, NCOs and drivers, instead of the mixture of Persian and Egyptian civilian drivers which the Government in Bombay insisted on providing. As the campaign was mounted from India, no element of the Military Train was made available, but Napier had appointed Major Warden, who had served in the Crimea with the Land Transport Corps, to organize an animal transport train for the campaign. However, it took several months of wrangling before the Bombay Government would agree to provide some properly organized and disciplined transport based on units available from the Punjab. By this time, before agreement was reached, a base was already being established at Zula, through the anchorage at Annesley Bay. This was selected by a reconnaissance party in September, and, soon after, the Sappers started on the construction of the lengthy piers that were necessary, and the building of the base began.

Although there was a considerable flow of animals into the base – camels, mules and horses which had been purchased from the Middle East, and as far afield as Spain, Italy and Turkey – there was by the end of October still no formed transport organization staff to receive them, and many ran wild and suffered from lack of food and water. The total number of animals received from Suez was 10,045 mules, 1,302 donkeys, 741 camels and, later, 2,641 mules from the Punjab. A total of 20,000 mules or pack bullocks and 8,000 camels was the force requirement. Although they had to be used at an early stage, the civilian muleteers were not properly controlled and totally lacking in responsibility or discipline.

The force was carried from India in 75 steam transports, 205 sailing transports, eight tugs and three small steamers. Nine of these vessels were transports provided by the British Indian Steam Navigation Company, who were to operate ships on behalf of the Army until the late 1960s. The size of these ships ranged from 650 tons to 1,659 tons, still very small compared with those to follow some twenty years later. There were also

three hospital ships, the *Golden Fleece*, the *Mauritius* and the *Queen of the South*. These each carried 420 patients in cots and 184 in hammocks. Later two more hospital ships were sent.

Initial landings from the fleet were made prematurely, troops being put ashore before the Commissariat were ready to maintain them or transport available to carry supplies and water forward. Other troops had to remain on the troopships in the considerable discomfort of the Red Sea heat, because facilities were not available ashore. All in all, for the first two months the situation was chaotic. The marine base which was vital, and the transport which was equally so, both suffered from poor and inadequate planning.

However, by January, 1868, things were looking better. The Sappers had built a tramway from one of the now completed piers in the bay to the camp at Zula. The projected railway from Zula to Kumayli had been started and one locomotive, out of six ordered, had been landed. The construction started slowly, under immense difficulties, but by March eight miles had been completed and six trains a day were carrying supplies. The railway, in fact, was never completed and ended ¾ of a mile short of Kumayli. However, with only three engines out of six received, during its operating period of March to May, 1868, it was worked intensively and successfully carried 14,000 troops, 10,000 followers, 9,000 tons of commissariat stores, 2,400 tons of material, and 2,000 tons of soldiers' baggage.

By January too, the organized military mule units from the Punjab had arrived and transport could be properly controlled. This was what had been required from the beginning and fortunately it was not too late for the main thrust by Napier before the rains were due at the end of January. Forty-four elephants were also brought in from India to take heavier loads, particularly artillery. For the main advance, it was now possible to divide the transport into a Highland and a Lowland animal train. The disciplined Punjab military drivers operated the Highland train from the top of the pass at Adigrat to Magdala, and were supplemented by infantry soldiers. The civilian drivers worked the route from the pass to the base at Zula. This system proved effective.

From a series of forward bases, Napier took his

force to Magdala and the fortress was assaulted and destroyed, with few casualties to the force. Theodore was killed in the attack and the captives released. It was a formidable march under extreme conditions, requiring great determination and endurance. Fortunately by then the transport and the commissariat were equal to the task, though the cost in animals was high. 41,000 animals were used in the operation, consisting of 18,000 mules, 1,500 ponies, 12,000 camels, 1,100 draught bullocks, 7,000 pack bullocks, 1,800 asses and 41 elephants. 7,000 animals died, but all but five of the elephants survived and were returned to India.

In this campaign, unlike the Crimean War or the China War, there appears to have been no real disagreement between the Commissariat and the Transport organization, over the control of transport, and, despite a confused start, a satisfactory working arrangement was made. Sir Robert Napier, once he had got the transport organization that he had originally asked for, like Wellington before him, made sure that it worked, and it served him well. It was still an *ad hoc* organization though, even if the need for a permanent establishment was recognized.

The Zulu War *1878–1879*

In July, 1878, the aggressiveness of the Zulu tribe led by Chief Cetewayo against the settlers in Natal caused a British Force to invade Zululand. This campaign is best remembered for one incident in January, 1879 – the defence of Rorke's Drift near the Tugela River. Victoria Crosses were awarded in this gallant action to eleven of the defenders of this small post of 140 strong, mainly of the 24th Regiment (The South Wales Borderers). They defeated and stemmed the advance of the Zulus, after one column of the British Force from the 24th Regiment had suffered a disaster at Isandhlwana, being overrun by the main Zulu Army. One of the VCs awarded was to Assistant

The Iron Girder Bridge, Kumalyi, Abyssinia, 1868, with train from Zula. The line and bridges were constructed by the Sappers for the campaign. (War Office Library, Ministry of Defence)

Supply waggon with twenty oxen, Zulu War, 1879. Similar teams were used by Colonel Harry Smith during the Kaffir War of 1854. At best these teams could cover about ten miles in one day. (IRCT)

Commissary James Langley Dalton of the Commissariat and Transport Corps for his part in actively superintending the work of defence, helping to stem the rush of the Zulus and saving the life of a soldier. He was severely wounded during the attack.

The campaign had started well, with the force, under the command of Lord Chelmsford, advancing in four columns from forward bases, and at this stage the animal transport system, including ox-waggon trains, worked well. Of particular interest is the use of the railways, which had developed considerably since the Kaffir War in 1834. The system, which was still expanding

and had reached Pietermaritzburg, was used extensively in building up the forward bases from the main base at Durban. There were no other technical developments in the land transport, and the animal transport was perfectly adequate and well organized, using about 12,000 oxen, horses and mules. After the almost total annihilation of the column before the Rorke's Drift action, operations were suspended for several months until reinforcements arrived from England between February and May, 1879, in the now even more rapid troopers. 387 officers and 8,895 men with 1,866 horses and 238 carriages were conveyed in twenty steamers. It is interesting to note that troopships under sail had now ceased to be used. However, even when the reinforcements arrived, some difficulty was experienced for a short time in providing them with sufficient transport. The loss at Islandhlwana proved hard to make up, and even more animals were required for the larger force. The shortage was successfully overcome, however, and, after some delay, mobility was restored. By July the power of the Zulus had been broken and peace was restored.

Overall, this campaign was well supported by its transport and commissariat organization, which, at this time, in the general reorganization still taking place, was combined. Indeed, the organization at Durban, which had been established under one head, Deputy Commissary General Young, was most effective. It was a model of its kind for the disembarkation of troops, animals and material, and was completely co-ordinated with the Royal Navy. It was to be the forerunner of similar operations in the future, though not all were to go so well.

Egypt and the Sudan *1882–1898*

Involvement in Egypt for the first time since 1801 was to mark the beginning of a period in an area where the British Army was to be found in strength for the next 75 years. It was also to be the first area in which the Army had a modern transport organization functioning in a series of campaigns. This is not to say that the organization was totally effective from the start. There was still to

Soldiers of 2nd Battalion, The Duke of Cornwall's Light Infantry moving up the River Nile, Sudan Campaigns, 1885–1898. (Regimental Museum, The Duke of Cornwall's Light Infantry)

Transshipping stores from railway to river. Steamer and nuggas move upstream towards Omdurman, Sudan Campaigns. (Museum of Army Transport, Beverley)

be much heated debate and considerable misunderstanding and misjudgement on the division of responsibilities. But it was to be the beginning of an era in which the need for a transport organization, now recognized, was progressively met.

Various campaigns took place during this period, but we shall concentrate on some of the types of transport used, and its effectiveness. The reason for a return to Egypt was, in the first place, to restore the legitimate ruler, Khedive Tewfik, who had been ousted as the result of a military coup led by Colonel Arabi Pasha. Throughout this period, apart from the railways, now being used extensively, there were no new types of land transport involving the new technologies in use in the area. But steam-driven ships and rivercraft were much in evidence. The force was carried in troop transports hired by both the Imperial and Indian Governments. Larger vessels were now to be seen, and many of the newest were of almost 5,000 tons, providing much improved facilities for the troops. The Suez Canal, opened in 1869,

was to be the centre of much military attention now and for the next hundred years.

The initial force landed in Egypt at Alexandria in July, 1882, under the command of General Sir Garnet Wolseley, and established a base at Ismailia. The force was 24,000 strong and had the aim of capturing Cairo as a prerequisite to restoring the Ruler. The Force had assigned to it eight companies of the newly designated Commissariat and Transport Corps, which, for a short while between 1869 and 1881, had the title Army Service Corps for the first time. This title would be restored again in 1888.

Although the Canal was quickly captured, it had been dammed by the enemy further south and the water level so reduced that the use of shipping and lighterage was restricted. Steam pinnaces were utilized on the Canal, but by no means filled the gap. The railway, too, could only be operated well below capacity, since the force at the beginning of the campaign only had access to limited rolling stock and few locomotives. There were hardly any additional mules available to make up this particular deficiency, and what rolling stock there was had to be used largely for troop movement. Sir Garnet Wolsely in fact landed more troops than his transport could support, and this was reflected in men going short of rations, due to sheer lack of ability to distribute them. However, his gamble paid off, as the larger strength of his force ashore ensured a rapid decision in the campaign, with the victory at Tel-el-Kebir. This was followed by the capture of additional locomotives and rolling stock, and the subsequent advance to Cairo was easily supported. Cairo was captured on 14 September and conditions in Egypt for a while returned to normal.

In 1884 the Sudan became the object of attention, as the Egyptian Army was unable to cope with the increasing power and aggressiveness of Mohammed Ali, who described himself as the Mahdi, with the divine power to release Sudan from its Egyptian oppressors.

In February 1884, a small British force was sent to Suakin, on the Red Sea, to oppose the Mahdi's uprising, but it was subsequently withdrawn after a few weeks, as it was clear that it would not achieve its aim. However, this had no special transport features, but arising from the expedition

was the decision to send General Charles Gordon as Governor of Sudan to rally the Egyptian forces and restore order.

The power of the Mahdi became increasingly violent as the year progressed and Gordon's position in Khartoum was seriously threatened. After much procrastination by the British Government, it was decided to send a force under the command of the now Lord Wolseley to restore the situation in Sudan and to rescue Gordon. From a transportation view alone, the launching of an expedition of the necessary size presented enormous problems. The route of advance selected, up the Nile, involved a line of communication of 1,400 miles. There are some transportation aspects which are special to this campaign, but involve no new technology. Although the use of the Nile as the line of advance and communication dictated the means of much of the transport, and boats were used to a large extent, there were obstacles to navigation beyond Aswan, in the form of the four cataracts. This involved tedious transfers of men and material from one type of transport to

Train on the Khartoum Railway with boat sections, Sudan Campaign. (Museum of Army Transport, Beverley)

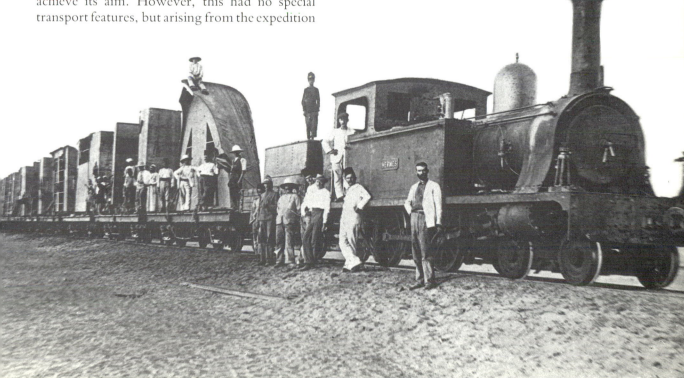

Sir Charles Wilson with escort of the Royal Sussex Regiment embarking at Gubat, 1885, Sudan Campaigns. (National Army Museum)

another. The railway, which was still incomplete, was available for some quite long sections of the route, but still involved transfers either on or off boats or camels, the only other form of transport. Eight hundred specially constructed whaleboats were used to move troops up the Nile and the logistic problems for this movement alone were not inconsiderable.

Part of the force, some 2,000 men, was sent across the desert from Korti, two hundred miles north of Khartoum, in an effort to reach there more quickly than the waterborne force, which had to follow the great bend in the Nile. It faced enormous difficulties which were exacerbated by not having sufficient camels for the task. In the event, it failed to reach Khartoum before the news of Gordon's death reached the force. It was withdrawn under great adversity, having suffered 300 casualties, and lost a large proportion of its 3,000 camels. In the meantime, an element of the waterborne force, in the shape of a small flotilla of two steam vessels under the command of Sir Charles Wilson, had reached Khartoum on 28

January, 1885, but, after receiving confirmation that Gordon was dead, was forced to retreat down the river again. They were indeed fortunate to escape, and their journey back, involving great navigational difficulties and constant attack from the shore, was extremely hazardous. When Wolseley received news of this disaster, he made plans for an initial advance with his force on Berber, but the Government would not agree to this or any further action. The whole force then withdrew in some disorder to Egypt and to the political and military storm that followed.

Throughout the whole operation the force had the support of a number of companies of the Commissariat and Transport Corps, which operated quite successfully within the limitations imposed on them. However, the Force Commander decided to appoint a Director of Transport responsible for all transport. This ran contrary to the new joint organization of the Commissariat and Transport Corps, combining supplies and transport. This decision by Lord Wolseley caused considerable confusion and for a lot of the time those on the ground contrived successfully to follow the system for which they had been trained. This is not the place to discuss the merits of either system; suffice it to say that in the eyes of some higher commanders there still remained uncertainty as to how transport should be organized and controlled, and its relationship with the supply system.

In this campaign, the officers of the Commissariat and Transport Corps operated the system they knew as best they could, and the failure of the expedition to rescue Gordon was not a reflection of any overall failings on their part, but of much broader issues.

The failure of the 1885 campaign in the Sudan was avenged later, in 1898, under General Kitchener's leadership, with the campaign successfully culminating in the battle of Omdurman and the reoccupation of Khartoum. The campaign provided a significant landmark in the building of military railways. Two Railway Companies of the Royal Engineers, trained in railway skills with the civil railways in England, were employed on the railways in Egypt and Sudan, to supplement the civil labour which had been working under the supervision of Royal Engineer officers. Their great achievement was the Sudan railway which they built across 232 miles of the Nubian Desert. In this last of the Egypt and Sudan campaigns in this period the railway played a vital part in the maintenance of the force and the successful conclusion to the campaign.

The Boer War 1899–1902

This long-drawn-out and bitter campaign, which used far more resources and went on for two years longer than most people predicted, is the first in which the British Army used mechanical road transport. As such, it is another important milestone in the changing means of transporting the Army. Apart from the actual introduction of mechanical road transport into the campaign,

which was operated by the Royal Engineers, the command and control of the main transport of the force was for the first time under one properly established organization. It was not as simple as it sounds, however, and, as Army Commanders changed, so did the ideas and the concept of the operation of the transport, irrespective of its created role and built-in capabilities.

Numerous changes took place in the newly constituted organization of the Army Service Corps which are not considered in detail, since only the transport aspects concern us. However, there were three important senior personalities concerned, not just with the overall command of the operations, but who also intervened personally in the operation of transport during the campaign. In this respect, they were all to a greater or lesser degree involved in the future of mechanical road transport.

The first to consider is Sir Redvers Buller, who, when Quartermaster General of the Army in 1887, took the decisive step to re-create the Army Service Corps (it had existed for a short period from 1869–1881) on a properly organized basis. This combined commissariat and transport in one militarized corps. It was on this basis, by companies, that 3,000 officers and men of the Army Service Corps were sent to South Africa during 1899–1900 to supervise, operate and control the supply and transport systems of the force, General Buller was by now himself Commander of the initial force in South Africa, and remained so until early in 1900, when the Army suffered some reverses and he was replaced by Lord Roberts. The strength of the force during Buller's time was about 60,000, but, by the end of the war, some 359,000 had been embarked from Britain and India. Six transport ships were used continuously between Britain and South Africa, and thirty-one from India to carry the troops, animals and stores required. The land transport requirement for this size of force, operating in such a huge area, was considerable. To meet this need, 347,000 horses, 104,000 mules and 2,000 mule waggons were added to the shipping bill in addition to the personnel. There was also a vast number of horses, mules and oxen, with carts, obtained locally, and the Army Service Corps drivers were supplemented by locally employed

TOP *Army steam road transport really began to develop during the 1880s and 1890s so that there was some expertise available at the beginning of the Boer War. Seen here is an Army Service Corps (ASC) Baggage Train on manoeuvres in 1893. Thirty-six tons of stores were carried from Aldershot to Liddington, Berkshire. The tractor is built by Aveling and Porter. The term steam 'Steam Sapper' previously used was discontinued in 1894 and thereafter the term 'Traction Engine' was used. (National Army Museum)*

ABOVE *2nd Battalion The Royal Fusiliers disembarking from SS **Pavonia** and entraining for the front. Cape Town, South Africa, Boer War, 1899–1902. (City of London Headquarters, The Royal Regiment of Fusiliers)*

ABOVE *Fowler traction engine and train fording a drift in the Transvaal. The traction engine in the foreground is a Burrell 224. (IRCT)*

LEFT *Fowler steam tractor with armour-plating protection for boiler, cylinder, fire-box and working parts, drawing howitzer and three armour-plated waggons. This kind of protection was much used during the Boer War. (IRCT)*

BELOW *Armoured Train Number 2, Boer War. (City of London Headquarters, The Royal Regiment of Fusiliers)*

personnel in each of their companies, to compete with the total number of animals involved.

When Lord Roberts assumed command, he took out from England with him General Kitchener as his Chief of Staff. Kitchener took over from Roberts at the end of 1900, when the war was thought to be over, but it was to drag on for another eighteen months, before Kitchener brought it to a successful conclusion. We shall return later to the part played by these two generals in relation to transport, but will first consider some of the transport itself.

In December, 1899, 45 Company Royal Engineers, equipped with steam traction engines, originally for Sapper tasks, was sent out to South Africa, Colonel J. B. L. Templer was appointed Director of Steam Road Transport, with a small staff. Initially 45 Company sailed with eleven traction engines, McLarens and Fowlers, and thirty-five trucks, but these were later built up to twenty-one traction engines, and two steam lurries (the original name for lorries), a Foden and a Thornycroft. The Company had its problems, caused by both the functioning of the vehicles and the tasks allotted to them by the Army Staff. These tasks frequently affected the performance of the vehicles. The Staff were totally inexperienced in the use of mechanical transport, and, consequently, the vehicles were not used within their proper capabilities and to their best advantage. They were put in mixed convoys with animal transport, and, moving at the animals' slow speed, consumed excessive water and fuel, which were in short supply on the veldt. Consequently, stocks of both had to be carried at the expense of some of the maintenance load. As the tractors were of mixed makes, design faults and spares were more difficult to deal with. Some conditions across country, such as sand, were a problem too, but they were always able to winch themselves and their trailers out of trouble if they bogged down. The Foden and Thornycroft 3-ton steam lurries, on the other hand, proved unsatisfactory outside the cantonment areas, because they were virtually inoperative off the roads. However, despite these initial shortcomings a vital start towards mechanization had been made.

R. E. B. Crompton, now a re-employed Lieutenant-Colonel commanding the Electrical Engineers (Volunteers) Corps, returns to the scene. Following his experience in India with steam engines in 1873, which at that time had been noted by Lord Roberts, Crompton was soon to become involved with him again. Roberts appointed him to organize an integrated steam tractor transport corps, from those with his unit as well as those with Colonel Templer. He also became an adviser to Lord Roberts on these vehicles, as well as operating them for general transport purposes. After the recovery of a bogged-down 12-ton gun of the Royal Field Artillery with his tractors, movement of artillery became standard practice. He later, to his amusement, got into trouble with General Kitchener for not only moving the guns, but for firing them at the enemy. Crompton returned home at the end of 1900, at Lord Robert's instigation, and was soon appointed to the main War Office committee to look at the development of mechanical transport for military purposes. There is no doubt that Lord Roberts was keen to progress with mechanical transport in the Army and he inspired Crompton to use his expertise and experience to help bring this about.

We must now turn to Lord Kitchener, who had very different ideas about transport. Having spent much of his service in the Middle East, he regrettably appeared to be somewhat ignorant of the new transport organization that had been delivered by Sir Redvers Buller, after such a long gestation period and with so many birth pangs. He also lacked an understanding of animal management. Nevertheless, he completely reorganized the allocation of transport in the force, in accordance with his own ideas, breaking down the allotted organization and pooling the transport. In so doing, he made the task of those who needed the transport and those that operated it all the harder. The fact that it was made to work at all was of much credit to those who were skilled in its operation.

The pooled system that was introduced placed too much of the animal management in unskilled and uncaring hands, and, as a result, the animal casualties were enormous. Of the total number of horses – 347,000, and 104,000 mules – well over 200,000 died, largely from misuse and starvation. The figures for oxen were not recorded, which is

Train moving over temporary bridge after the Boers had destroyed the main structure. (Museum of Army Transport, Beverley)

perhaps just as well as they would have presented a dismal picture: the deaths were certainly in excess of the horses and mules. The stench of dead animals round Pretoria was all-pervading, and so many baggage animals died every day that, without Crompton's detachment of tractors and trailers in 1900, the distribution of rations in that area might have failed. The dead animals also contaminated the water supplies and one of the jobs given to Crompton with his tractors was to drag the bodies which littered the roads away from water sources.

Mention must now be made of the railways, which were used extensively for moving personnel and supplies, when the lines had not been blocked by the Boers. Without the use of the railways, maintenance of the force over the long distances involved would not have been possible. From all four of the ports used by the British – Durban, East London, Port Elizabeth and Cape Town – main lines ran north and converged on Pretoria. Armoured trains were used to defend the lines and to protect the troops and stores carried. In spite of this, the lines were sabotaged by the Boers. By this time the Royal Engineer railway units were quite well established, training having started in the 1880s with the London,

Chatham and Dover Railway. As a result, by the start of the Boer War 8 Company Royal Engineers had been infiltrated into the Cape Government Railways and was able to assist in their operation from an early stage. Hospital trains were specially constructed, or adapted from normal stock, and were very effective and used extensively for evacuation. They were a link to hospital ships which plied between Durban and the UK. Ordinary trains were also used to carry less serious cases. The types of road transport used for the evacuation of casualties, however, fell short of what could have been expected by this time, and seemed to have progressed little. Because of the cutback in the allocation of transport, unsprung ox carts, open to all weather, were often used, and subjected the wounded to most uncomfortable journeys. Crompton's tractors and open trailers were also used to bring back wounded, and he himself was critical of the way in which they had to travel.

A form of transport new to the battlefield was to make its appearance at this time – the bicycle. It

The bicycle was now an accepted form of military transport. Cyclist messengers at Lord Methuen's Headquarters, 1900, Boer War. (National Army Museum)

was mainly used for orderlies to carry messages, but a more ambitious use was introduced. This was a rail tandem, which consisted of a number of cycles fixed together, and fitted with lightweight flanged wheels. They provided transport for scouts who used the railway lines to cover greater distances more easily on their patrols. Bicycles were to survive as personal transport in the Army in various roles for many years to come.

Mention has been made of the numbers of troops and animals carried in the now all steam-ship troopers from both the United Kingdom and India to South Africa. These vessels provided the highest standards of speed and comfort so far achieved for troopships, even though they were, as always, crammed to capacity. The vessels em-

ployed were nearly all requisitioned passenger liners, and this was now standard practice. The vessels mostly came from lines that had been involved with the Army for fifty years or more – P & O, Bibby, British India and Cunard – with Union, Castle, and White Star for rather less a period. Most were between 5,000 and 10,000 tons, though the first ship to disembark at the Cape was the Castle liner *Roslin Castle* of 4,267 tons. She carried a battalion of the Duke of Wellington's Regiment, and had left Southampton with the first convoy of reinforcements on 20

Horse-drawn ambulances, Boer War. (IRCT)

October, 1899. General Sir Redvers Buller, on his way to be Commander-in-Chief, left Southampton on 14 September in another Castle ship, the *Dunottar Castle*. A fellow passenger on the ship was the correspondent of the *Morning Post*, Mr Winston Churchill. A few months later, the Castle and Union lines were to amalgamate to form the Union-Castle Mail Steamship Company.

During the war P & O built three vessels specially for trooping, *Assaye*, *Plassy* and *Sobraon*. These were twin-screw steamers of 7,400 tons, and had a speed of 16 knots. P & O carried some 150,000 troops in nine ships during the war, but BI were the largest providers of ships for trooping, with thirty-seven vessels involved. Bibby continued to build ships which were taken over as troopers during the war, and many went on to become well known in the First World War. The vessels of these shipping lines were to become very familiar to thousands of British and Colonial troops in two World Wars.

The war had been a tremendously hard training ground for the Army, showing up all its strengths and weaknesses. At its end, as far as transportation was concerned, the main land transport operators, the Army Service Corps, reverted to the far-reaching organization carefully planned by General Buller before the war. This was subsequently adjusted to take account of the introduction of mechanical transport, which was now becoming an established fact. Animal transport was by no means obsolete, but it now had both a rival and a partner.

Before the Boer War was over, serious studies into the future use of mechanical transport in the Army had been started by the War Office. The Mechanical Transport Committee was formed in 1900, and in December of that year four sub-committees were established – Experimental and Motor, Royal Artillery, Royal Engineers, and Army Service Corps. The work of this Committee will be considered in the next chapter, together with the civilian developments, which by this time were making considerable progress.

Royal Engineer Balloon detachment drawn by a team of oxen, Boer War. (School of Transportation, RCT)

Pack yak of the British Military Mission, Ladak, Tibet, 1904. The yak can carry a load of 200 pounds for fifteen miles a day at a height of 15,000 feet. (IRCT)

3

The Emergence of

Mechanical Transport

ALTHOUGH EXPERIMENTS with steam tractors had been made prior to and during the Boer War with limited success, it was the establishment of the Mechanical Transport Committee, mentioned at the end of the last chapter, which was to be the turning point in the great changes to take place in transporting the Army on land. The Committee had been given considerable powers, both to compare the relative merits of steam and internal combustion engines and to experiment with and recommend the most suitable vehicles for the Army's use. They were also to decide who were to drive the vehicles for the overall maintenance support of the Army, including ambulances and staff cars, (as distinct from vehicles allocated to regiments solely for use on unit tasks). It was agreed that the Army Service Corps (ASC) should be responsible for the operation of this transport. In 1903 an Inspectorate of Mechanical Transport was also established within the ASC to deal with the technical aspects of MT, and to act as technical advisers at the War Office on MT. One of its officers was also on the MT Committee. These were essential steps in the process of mechanizing the Army.

The Committee had remarkable unanimity in most of its work, the only major hesitation being caused by the pronounced reluctance within the Army to discard the steam engine in favour of the petrol internal combustion engine (the IC engine). This was mainly because there were some doubts about the availability of petrol in the event of war, and some concern over its safe handling.

Paraffin as a fuel was widely considered, but, despite extensive experiments, with which Colonel Crompton was again involved, a satisfactory engine to accept it could not be produced. It did, however, continue to be used as a fuel for steam engines. By 1911 doubts about petrol had been cast aside. Satisfactory civilian usage, and the wide range of trials of vehicles, including results from manœuvres both in the United Kingdom and on the Continent, convinced all concerned that petrol should replace steam for Army vehicles. In field units steam engines were immediately replaced with IC-engine vehicles. Base units retained steam engines until they could be phased out and similarly replaced, though this was not until during the First World War when they had a mixture of both.

In 1902 the first light four-seater car had been purchased by the MT Committee for trials by the General Officer Commanding 1 Corps at Aldershot. This trial was the responsibility of the local Commander ASC, and the car was driven by an ASC driver. It was to be the forerunner of the modern staff car, soon to become a familiar and essential part of the Army. The fact that the Army now had a properly trained and organized Corps to accept responsibility on the ground for the new mechanical transport as it appeared was of considerable importance. In a few short years a number of dedicated and enlightened officers had turned the tide of uncertainty and mistrust that had been threatening the efficient operation of its transport. They were helped by a now supportive

Government. It was also encouraging at this time that a very much closer liaison had been established between the Army and civilian vehicle manufacturers, and this was to establish the pattern for the future and to influence the Army's choice of vehicles and their operation. The illustrations to this chapter and their accompanying explanatory captions, although not exhaustive, give some idea of the wide range of vehicles considered by the MT Committee during this period, and of some of those selected for operational use.

8 Horse-power, two-cylinder horizontal-engine Wolseley outside the War Office, Whitehall, London, 1902. The passengers are, left to right, Field-Marshal HRH The Duke of Connaught, Sir J. G. Maxwell and Captain W. F. Lascelles, Scots Guards. The driver is Corporal Clements, ASC. (IRCT)

TOP 8 Horse-power Panhard Levassor. Seated on the left is Lieutenant-General J. D. P. French with members of his staff and an ASC driver, Aldershot, Hampshire, 1904. (IRCT)

ABOVE German Milnes-Daimler five-ton lorry Number 16 of the ASC, 1905. The driver is Driver E. J. Grubb, ASC. (IRCT)

In 1908/1909 three troop movement trials, independent of the work of the MT Committee, were conducted in conjunction with civilian organizations, and might be considered as important landmarks in this aspect of transportation. These trials gave publicity to the scope for larger-scale troop movement by mechanical transport and were contrasting in the types of vehicles involved. The first were steam-driven omnibuses, the second petrol-driven omnibuses, and the third petrol-driven cars and commercial lorries. The first move was carried out in December, 1908, when a mobilization exercise of the 5th Battalion, Essex Regiment (Territorial Army) took place. A company of 120 men was moved on the initiative of the Company Commander in two hired Clarkson Steamers – 32 hp paraffin-burning steam-engined buses. Even overloaded as they were, they covered the 14 miles from Chelmsford to Lashingdon over mud roads in just over an hour. Although only a small move, it was a valuable and encouraging test at the time. The second, later in the month, was larger and more official. Under the orders of the GOC Eastern Command, 24 petrol-driven omnibuses were hired from the London General Omnibus Company and were used to convey 500 troops of the Norfolk and Essex Regiments from London to Shoeburyness. Again, in those early days, it was a successful experiment, and no doubt helped the pro-petrol protagonists.

BELOW *Mechanical transport of 77 Company ASC at Curragh Camp, Ireland. The motor car second from the left is a Clement Talbot, the others are Wolseleys. (IRCT)*
RIGHT *Troops moving by motor omnibus. The first occasion on which this took place was in December, 1908. A larger-scale move took place later that month when twenty-four London omnibuses moved 500 men of 1st Battalion, The Norfolk Regiment and 3rd Battalion, The Essex Regiment from London to Shoeburyness, Essex, via Warley, Essex. (British Library)*

The third of these trials was organized by the Automobile Association on a rather grander and more public scale, with the blessing and attendance of the great reforming Secretary of State for War, R. B. Haldane. This involved a composite battalion of the Grenadier, Coldstream and Scots Guards, with their arms and personal kit, and, in addition, all the battalion equipment. On 17 March, 1909, they were conveyed from London to Hastings and back in 316 privately-owned and -driven civilian cars of various makes. Some thirty civilian-driven commercial-type lorries were used to carry the battalion's equipment. This highly successful event, although not of a tactical nature, ensured that much publicity was given to the effective use of mechanical transport in moving troops.

In 1907 the first mechanical transport unit had been formed, in conformity with the policy produced by the MT Committee. This was 77 Company Army Service Corps, and others gradually followed. In 1909 a reduction was made in the number of horse transport units of the ASC, and they were replaced by MT companies. When mechanical transport was introduced, the Army Ordnance Department was made responsible for all vehicle repairs other than running repairs, which remained the responsibility of the ASC for its own vehicles. There was an adjustment in workshop allocation between the two Corps and various designs of mobile workshop and recovery vehicles were considered to meet the new requirement. It was not, in fact, until after the start of the First World War that the most suitable vehicles were produced for this task.

Once the IC-engined vehicle was accepted for service in 1911, steps were taken to ensure that the Army vehicles were as compatible as possible with those needed on the civilian market. Some degree of standardization was also achieved

First move of troops by motor car, St Patrick's Day, 17 March, 1909. At the invitation of the Automobile Association (AA), members of the Grenadier, Coldstream and Scots Guards were motored in members' cars from London to Hastings, Kent, sixty miles in under four hours. The vehicle marked E 48 in the column on Polehill, Sevenoaks, Kent, is a Brasier. (Automobile Association)

between the various manufacturers of the Army's vehicles, and the first buy of 1,400 lorries were so designed that many parts were interchangeable between the different makes. This simplified the supply of spares and the repair system. Agreement having been reached with the automobile manufacturers to produce certain types of vehicle that were both, in essentials, suitable for military and civilian use, a subsidy was paid to civilian owners of such lorries on the agreement that the vehicles would be handed over to the Army on mobilization. This was a far-reaching and enterprising idea, which, after some early setbacks, and consequent adjustment to the provisional scheme, worked well.

However, an even greater number of vehicles was required on mobilization than could be provided by the subsidy scheme, and it was also necessary to introduce an impressment scheme for other types of civilian-owned vehicles to make up the deficiency. This complicated the provision of spares and the repair system, but the scheme was well planned and supervised from the start, and the British Expeditionary Force was not short of transport or the ability to maintain it on mobilization.

So it was that by the outbreak of the First World War in 1914, although the British Army, like the German, was still dependent for much of its tactical land movement on animal transport, the foundations of mechanization had been firmly laid. The British Expeditionary Force went to France with mechanical transport, the IC-engined lorry in particular, in quantities that it hardly seemed possible to have produced in the time since the MT Committee made its recommendations in 1911. The numbers and types of vehicle were to increase dramatically and were used in every theatre. The Army was also going to war with a properly established logistic transport organization – the ASC. It appeared to have none of the disadvantages of its predecessors.

Railways, with their vast expansion worldwide, were to be used extensively, both to move troops and supplies, and for casualty evacuation. Construction and operation of railways by the Royal Engineers, including light railways in the forward areas, was also to be widespread, and

Baggage of the Guards units ascending Riverhill, near Tonbridge, Kent, 17 March, 1909. (Automobile Association)

inland water transport, for which the Royal Engineers were also responsible, used in a variety of ways. Movement by sea was to involve both the Royal Navy and civilian-operated transports. They carried the Army both in the normal trooping role and in the assault role. Our next chapter therefore brings together in the First World War all forms of transportation for moving the Army, with a full range of the new mechanical transport.

Although the military aeroplane was to appear in its combat role in 1914, its use for troop or supply movement for the Army was not introduced until after the war.

ABOVE *Crossley light truck c1912. (Leo Cooper Collection)*

BELOW *Foden steam tractors, 1912. (IRCT)*

4

1914–1918

The First World War

Background

Britain entered the First World War with its Army in a state of preparedness that only ten years earlier few would have judged possible. Overall, this remarkable achievement was very much due to the resolute action taken by the Secretary for War, R. B. Haldane (later Lord Haldane), who, with General Haig to help him at the War Office, implemented the sweeping recommendations of the Esher Report, published in 1904. The post of Commander-in-Chief was abolished, the Army Council was established, and a proper functional Staff system introduced. As a result the War Office, with the General Staff, became an extremely efficient instrument to give impetus to the complete reorganization of the Army. Operational training was updated and made realistic and the administrative structure of both the Regular Army and the Reserve Army was fundamentally changed.

The work of the Mechanical Transport Committee considered in the last chapter was an essential part of this dynamic drive to modernize and re-equip the Army. The Committee's contribution was to transform its means of transportation. Not only was a considerable advance made in producing well-tested mechanical transport in effective quantities, but there was also now a well-trained, acceptable organization to operate it. Nevertheless, despite the impressive quantity of mechanical transport that was available when war was declared on 4 August, 1914, the British

Expeditionary Force's (BEF) road transport needs in France were still met in large part by animal transport. Although the quantities of mechanical transport increased enormously during the war, animals still continued to be employed in vast numbers throughout. This situation also existed in operations outside Europe, but it was only in the operations in Mesopotamia, Egypt and Palestine that the mobility that mechanical transport offered was significantly attainable. As will be seen, though, mechanical and animal transport operated together in all theatres, and their usage was at last being properly co-ordinated, even under widely varying conditions.

Throughout the war railways in one form or another were a vital method of transportation for both men and materiel. The Royal Engineers were by this time fully established in railway matters, and the extent of their involvement can be gauged by the fact that almost 2,000 officers and 66,000 men were railway-trained and sent overseas during the war. In France, where the civilian railway system was used extensively, static conditions applied for most of the campaign there. In that situation it was possible to carry large numbers of troops from the Channel ports to forward areas, as well as laterally, and railways provided the main means of casualty evacuation to rearward hospitals or to the ports. The bulk of the maintenance requirements for the Army was also carried by rail from the bases to railheads established well forward. From there distribution to units was by animal or mechanical transport of the ASC. In France there was relatively little day-to-day enemy ground interference with the railways, but this was not always so elsewhere. However, the railheads in France were not invulnerable to shelling and for the last two years of the war air attacks were also made on the railway system. Some major enemy advances threatened, but did not seriously hinder, its operation until the main German offensive in 1918. Other factors did, however, and there was a serious rolling stock and track maintenance problem due to the excessive work load. This and other particular aspects of the railways are dealt with under each campaign.

Although in the case of the BEF much troop movement could take place from the UK by cross-channel ferry, there was a widespread use of the now larger troopships both for this movement and the continuing movement of the Army between India and France and the other theatres. The Gallipoli campaign provided an example of amphibious operations using warships and transports, whilst inland water transport was used extensively in Europe, in the Middle East and in Africa. Animals were transported in great numbers, from as far afield as Australia and India, and

the vastly improved ships and speed of movement reduced the transit casualty rates which had formerly been so much of a problem.

Women for the first time were to be found driving Service vehicles. In the UK, under the auspices of the Women's Legion, led by Lady Londonderry, they drove cars, ambulances, vans and motor cycles, and were initially attached to ASC Mechanical Transport (MT) Companies. Later they had their own organization, directly under the War Office. In an active service role in France and Belgium, the First Aid Nursing Yeomanry (FANY) drove motor ambulances and were the first women drivers serving overseas.

Not every theatre or campaign in this widespread war is considered in this chapter since some add little to the general theme of this book. This does not necessarily discount them as militarily unimportant, and indeed some have been included that are of lesser importance than those excluded, but are more widely illustrative of transportation.

Railway box waggons arriving on cross-channel ferry, France, 1914. (Imperial War Museum)

France and Belgium *1914–1918*

Because of the nature of the war in France and Belgium, with a long period when the front was stabilized, many of the illustrations of this campaign have been grouped by types of transportation, rather than in chronological order. This provides a better indication of the developments that took place over the whole period.

The initial strength of the BEF consisted of six infantry divisions and a cavalry division, together with supporting army and line of communication troops. The logistic transport units of the ASC were made up of thirty-four horse and nineteen mechanical transport companies, these numbers giving some indication of the high proportion of animal transport that still existed. ASC transport within divisions were known as Divisional Trains. Some 950 lorries and 250 cars accompanied the Force. These included vehicles obtained under the subsidy scheme, as well as impressed vehicles, as described in the last chapter.

Some impressed lorries went to France still in their old commercial livery, and within six weeks of the war starting, omnibuses from the London

General Omnibus Company were to be seen on the French and Belgian roads. They were still in their familiar red London General livery. Fifty volunteer drivers and their buses went to support the Royal Marines in the first batch at only one day's notice, and eventually some two thousand buses and their drivers, then enlisted, were used in France. One of their early tasks was to carry volunteers of the London Scottish, the first Territorial Army soldiers to go into action in France, to the First Battle of Ypres. Troop-carrying vehicles were now a fully recognized requirement for the rapid concentration of the infantry. Omnibuses, later added to with adapted lorries, were formed into the Auxiliary Omnibus Park, Army Service Corps, with 650 vehicles. This was capable of the rapid deployment of the marching troops of a Division in one lift. For its services in the final advance in 1918 the unit was Mentioned in Despatches by the Commander-in-Chief, the only ASC unit to receive this honour.

Unloading stores at Le Havre, France, 1914. Foden steam lorry and Dennis petrol lorries. (IRCT)

ABOVE *An impressed Leyland removal van outside the Cloth Hall, Ypres, Belgium, before any shelling had taken place, October, 1914. (Imperial War Museum)*

RIGHT *Daimler 30 cwt lorry. Seventy-five were impressed from the Tramway (MET) Omnibus Company and sent to France in 1914. (IRCT)*

BELOW *An impressed Harrods lorry awaiting repair at a workshop in France. (National Army Museum)*

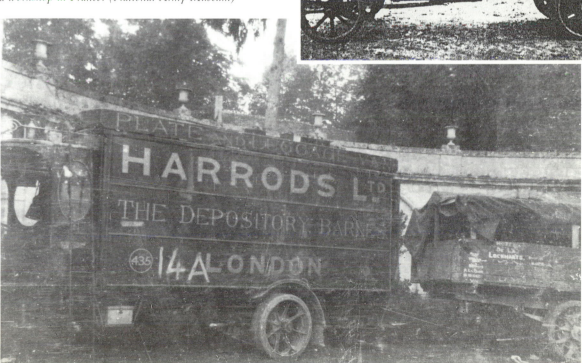

The smoothness and efficiency with which the mobilization and the move of the BEF to France took place is an indication of the success of the planning under the reorganized Staff system, and the training of those responsible on the ground. Movement to the Channel ports and from the ports of disembarkation in France and Belgium to the concentration area at Maubeuge were by rail. The overall movement took 14 days and during this time 1,400 special trains were used to convey troops to the ports. At Southampton they arrived every 12 minutes for 16 hours a day during these two weeks. The timing of trains both in the UK and in France was a vital part of the mobilization plan. Although a change of destination for the BEF in France was mooted by the War Office, the railway timetables were inexorable and a major factor in agreeing with the French to adhere to the original strategic plan.

The initial sea crossing, with a minimal enemy threat, presented little difficulty. However, the early loss of the use of the ports in Belgium, followed by a precautionary move of the bases at Boulogne and Le Havre, caused transportation problems with the transfer of the maintenance stores to new ports of disembarkation further west. These were, however, successfully overcome and some 60,000 tons of stores and 1,500 animals were moved in nine days to their new location at St Nazaire.

The retreat from Mons during the period of 13 days from 23 August, 1914, involved the infantry fighting and marching for some 200 miles to reach the south-east of Paris. Practically no mechanical transport was available at this stage for lifting any of the troops, and what there was had to be fully employed in sustaining the force during the withdrawal. After the front had been stabilized north of the River Aisne, following the successful but unexploited Battle of the Marne, the British infantry were moved by rail to the area of Ypres, in Flanders. When the First Battle of Ypres, which began on 20 October, ended, real mobility ceased, and trench warfare, with all the discomforts and horrors that it involved, became the lot of the British infantry in France and Flanders until the summer of 1918. Although the resupply of the forward troops once the front line was virtually static generally enabled the transportation system

to follow a set pattern, it was far from being a routine matter. Movement to the forward areas along devastated, shell-pocked roads targeted by the enemy artillery, and often by machine-gun fire as well, was a hazardous business, and much movement could only take place at night.

By mid-September, 1914, there were some 100,000 animals helping to support the Force of 240,000 British and 25,000 Indians in the forward areas. Horse and mule transport, including pack animals, was still often able to move more easily in the forward areas, where roads were little better than mud rivers in wet weather. Animals were used across the whole range of logistic transport requirements, from troop-carrying vehicles to ambulances. As pack animals, with a load of one hundred and eighty pounds, they carried everything from ammunition to water, as they had always done. The speed and flexibility of mechanical transport, though, was becoming apparent even to the most hardened animal supporter. While mobility was not greatly tested in France and Flanders, it was quite evident that the capability was there, and that the cross-country performance of mechanical vehicles would be improved.

Mention has been made of the evacuation of casualties by rail, but this was probably the easiest part of the casualty evacuation system, though there were delays to hospital trains because of congestion on the railways. A shortage of hospital trains also meant that ordinary rolling stock often had to be used, which could preclude the carriage of medical staff, and consequently a lack of treatment for patients on the journey. Nevertheless, the most difficult aspect was getting the casualty

TOP *Column of thirty ASC vehicles driving through a force of German cavalry after refusing to surrender during the retreat from Mons, Belgium, in August, 1914. Only two vehicles were lost. Painting by David Cobb. (IRCT)*

CENTRE *Horse-drawn TCV, 1914. This appears to be only a minor advance over a period of 130 years since the military fly of 1798. See illustration page 25. (IRCT)*

BOTTOM *Pack horses taking up ammunition near Bapaume, France, during operations on the Ancre, January, 1917. (IRCT)*

ABOVE *Holt tractors drawing 8-inch howitzers on the Albert Road, Amiens, France, September, 1916. (Imperial War Museum)*

LEFT *Although designed for towing heavy guns, the Holt tractor was used for other tasks, in this case drawing engineer stores. (IRCT)*

BELOW *A Foster Daimler tractor drawing box waggons on the Albert Road, Amiens. (IRCT)*

TOP *Lorries collecting ammunition at railhead. (IRCT)*

ABOVE *Troops moving up in barges on the Furness–
Dunkirk canal, Belgium, Battle of Ypres, 1914.
(Imperial War Museum)*

ABOVE *Water tank lorry, believed to be an impressed Wolseley, delivering to a roadside water point in a forward area. The H20 sign on the rear of the truck was the sign of 4 Water Tank Company ASC. (IRCT)*

RIGHT *The Army Postal Service at work. An AEC lorry of 74th Division collecting mail from a Field Post Office. (IRCT)*

BELOW *2nd Guards embussing in lorries, Arras, France, 1917. (IRCT)*

from where he was wounded or became sick to the regimental aid post, and thence back by ambulance to the advanced dressing stations, for further treatment and evacuation to a railhead. There often had to be much improvisation in the movement of casualties in the forward areas, since not only did the number of casualties at times swamp the normal means, but the ground conditions were also generally appalling.

The casualty figures for the 1st Division at the First Battle of Ypres are indicative of the terrible toll inflicted by modern weapons in the type of warfare which was to be followed in Flanders for the next four years. The strength of the Division was reduced from some 18,000 all ranks to 68 officers and 2,776 other ranks. The evacuation and treatment of such numbers of casualties, and there was worse to come, presented enormous problems for the Royal Army Medical Corps (RAMC) and those responsible for their transportation. The ASC drove all the ambulances, either animal or MT, and formed part of the RAMC unit to which they were attached. The sort of conditions under which the medical staff and the ambulance drivers operated can be indicated by the citation for the award of the Victoria Cross to Private Richard George Masters, ASC, attached to 141 Field Ambulance, RAMC:

'For most conspicuous bravery and devotion to duty. Owing to an enemy attack, communications were cut off, and wounded could not be evacuated. The road was reported impassable, but Private Masters volunteered to try to get through, and after the greatest difficulty, succeeded, although he had to clear the road of all sorts of debris. He made journey after journey throughout the afternoon, over a road consistently shelled and swept by machine-gun fire, and was on one occasion bombed by an aeroplane. The greater part of the wounded cleared from this area were evacuated by Private Masters, as his was the only car that got through at this particular time.'

Evacuating casualties using an aerial ropeway. (Museum of Army Transport)

ABOVE *Transporting wounded by mule-drawn trolley on the light railway from Crucifix Corner to Aveluy, October, 1916. (IRCT)*

RIGHT *Horse-drawn sledges used for the conveyance of wounded over muddy ground, Le Sans, October, 1916. (Imperial War Museum)*

BELOW *Men of the Middlesex Regiment returning from the trenches with their wounded in carts near Albert, Belgium, September, 1916. (IRCT)*

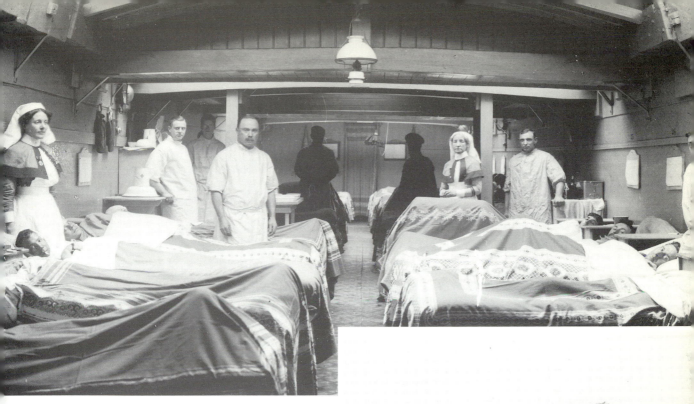

ABOVE *Canal barge similar to that shown on page 87 converted to carry casualties. (Imperial War Museum)*

RIGHT *A horse-drawn ambulance from a field ambulance (advanced hospital) near Oullers, September, 1916. (Imperial War Museum)*

BELOW *Standard railway coaches used for casualty evacuation at Dernancourt, September, 1916. (Imperial War Museum)*

Interior of a hospital train. (Imperial War Museum)

Miss Franklin and three members of First Aid Nursing Yeomanry (FANY) with their Napier Ambulances. (Imperial War Museum)

The 11th Battalion, The Durham Light Infantry moving up by light railway, Pilckem Ridge, 1917. (Leo Cooper Collection)

Embussing in boarded-up AEC/Daimler London omnibuses, Arras, 1917. (Imperial War Museum)

By 1918 the amount of mechanical transport with the BEF had been built up to 33,500 lorries, 1,400 tractors, 13,800 motor cars and many thousands of motor-cycles. The types and makes had increased considerably, so only a few can be shown in the illustrations. As the types and numbers increased, so the provisioning and repair system became more complex. An early change was made when responsibility for the total repair of all mechanical transport vehicles was returned from the Ordnance Department to the Army Service Corps workshops. This undoubtedly helped in the assimilation of the now very large fleet of vehicles. Other changes in the distribution of mechanical transport and animal transport were to take place during the overall period of the campaign, but, unlike past campaigns, these were carefully planned and implemented.

In 1916 there was an acute shortage of infantry manpower for the BEF, and the effect of Kitchener's planned build-up of BEF to seventy divisions was yet to be fully realized. The transportation system was by then so effective, when considered against the needs in a static situation, that a reduction was called for to assist the ever-growing requirement for front-line troops. At this stage the ASC manpower involved with transport was some 32,000 with animals and 54,000 with MT. As a result of reducing the transport and some of the supply element within the divisions, over 20,000 ASC personnel were made available to serve with the infantry and this they did with considerable success.

By 1917 there was serious concern about the state of the French civilian railway system which was in danger of breaking down due to over-usage. The French Railways were a vital part of the BEF's logistic system and the British Army Railway Operating Division, Royal Engineers, had some 75,000 personnel working with the French railways and assisting in their operation and control. A large number were trained railwaymen direct from the UK railways; others had been trained within the Royal Engineers. They were also involved in construction and repair of the system, both on main lines and on light railways in the forward area. Many miles were

Supply train steaming into railhead at Frenchincourt, March 1917. (Imperial War Museum)

TOP *Tank trains standing in Plateau station awaiting despatch to forward detraining railhead for the Cambrai offensive, 1917. (Imperial War Museum)*

ABOVE *Gun-carrier tank used for carrying supplies at Bucquoy, 19 August, 1918. (Imperial War Museum)*

LEFT *Maintaining bicycles under difficulties, Entreillers, 20 April, 1917. (Imperial War Museum)*

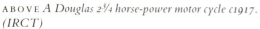

ABOVE *A Douglas 2¾ horse-power motor cycle c1917.*
(IRCT)

TOP *A bicycle unit passing through Brie, 1917.*
(National Army Museum)

RIGHT *Teleferica ropeway carrying supplies for XIV*
British Corps near Rochette, northern Italy, during the
winter campaign, 1917–1918. Not covered in the text.
(Imperial War Museum)

BELOW *HM King George V and HRH The Prince of*
Wales visiting the Duchess of Sutherland's hospital,
Calais, 14 June, 1917. An ASC-driven Rolls Royce
staff car. (Imperial War Museum)

built to link the trench systems and to provide sidings in the maintenance areas. They were responsible for operating some 800 miles of line. Since the maintenance system for the BEF depended on the use of the railway, disruption by enemy action or operating failures could have a serious effect. Steps were therefore taken to build up a reserve of mechanical transport to replace any part of the railway system, should it become necessary.

The ASC logistic transport in the Divisional Trains, and in Corps and Army had been based on a commodity system, with each transport company only carrying one type of load, such as ammunition or rations. This system was scrapped and companies re-allocated on a carefully controlled general transport pool system, carrying whatever type of load was necessary. In the event this reorganization saved the situation, and when the railways were interrupted during the retreat and subsequent advance of 1918, the new road system was able to take over. This regrouping of transport could with advantage have taken place earlier, since the old commodity system, with the situation existing within the BEF, was both uneconomical in transport and manpower. But the operation of MT was a new feature in the Army's maintenance system and everyone was still learning. The fact that there was a successful response to a new situation was a measure of lessons well learned.

The German offensive of March, 1918, was directed against some of the vital railway centres, and some lateral lines were overrun. Also, as the Germans advanced, their artillery was able to interfere more with the effective operation of the railways. However, the ASC mechanical transport units, now reorganized, were able to fill the gap, and continued to do so during the subsequent advance to victory from August until the Armistice in November.

Miss Laura May Chapman, FANY, at the wheel of a Sunbeam staff car, c1915. (Mrs D. Bremner-Milne)

Mesopotamia *November 1914 –*
November 1918

This campaign, mounted in November, 1914, by the Indian Government, with the original aim of protecting the Persian oilfields from the Turks, started only three months later than the operations on the Western Front. It is a campaign that often gets scant attention in military histories, although some 450,000 British and Indian soldiers were eventually involved. This is no doubt because it was far removed from the Western Front and achieved little towards easing the pressure there. However, from a transportation point of view it offers considerable interest, as extremes of both failure and achievement were clearly displayed. The force initially came from the Indian Army. It had its normal percentage of British Infantry regiments but no British Army logistic organization. The organization of transport and supplies until 1916 was in the hands of the Indian Army Supply and Transport Corps, who, although well geared for North-West Frontier warfare, were out of their depth when confronted with the situation in Mesopotamia. Furthermore, as so often in the past, they received tardy help from the Indian Government.

It was a campaign in which mobility ultimately produced success, but this did not start to happen until the conduct of the campaign, including control of its administration, was taken over by the War Office in February, 1916. Until that time the operations suffered from the sort of logistic problems so often inherent in the Indian Government's performance in the past when involved with campaigns outside India. It was a campaign necessitating movement and re-supply over long distances. Because of the grim, unhealthy climatic conditions, difficult terrain and lack of any amenities, it required a logistic understanding and implementation of a high order. Regrettably, until the War Office took over, it received neither, and the administration of the force during the first eighteen months was almost a total disaster.

During this time the strength of the force built up to five infantry divisions and one cavalry division, all of which were deficient in transport. An advance by a force under the command of Sir John Nixon was made up the River Tigris as far as Kut, with very slender logistic support, in the heat of the summer of 1915. Subsequently a

A light mosquito-proof ambulance drawn by mule, Mesopotamia, c1918. (IRCT)

1/4 Battalion, The Dorset Regiment embarking from the bank of the River Euphrates en route for Hit, Mesopotamia, 1918. (Leo Cooper Collection)

further advance to Ctesiphon was undertaken by General Townsend's Division in November, 1915, but an attack on the Turkish positions there was unsuccessful, and he was forced to withdraw to Kut. There he was besieged by the Turks. In April, 1916, after three unsuccessful and costly attempts at relief, Townsend was forced to capitulate with 12,000 men. The overall logistic arrangements on which these operations depended were totally inadequate and health and feeding standards deplorable. Soldiers were often at near starvation level, and the land and water transport, upon which the distribution of all maintenance depended, lacked in quantity, control and effectiveness.

The natural communications of Mesopotamia are by river, but the Indian Government failed to meet the obvious requirement for an adequate number of the right sort of boats, though they had been asked for. Also, Basra, the port of entry, and a thoroughly unhealthy place, had very limited berthing facilities, or indeed facilities of any sort, and, without constructing additional jetties, was incapable of efficient handling of the incoming maintenance for the force. All ships had to be unloaded in the stream and this could take over a month for each one. Although a request had been made to India by the Commander-in-Chief to extend the railway which ran from Basra for only 75 miles along the line of the River Tigris, this was rejected. Last in this list of transportation inadequacies was the almost total lack of mechanical transport in any form, for maintenance, the medical services or troop carrying.

When the War Office took over operations from the Indian Government in 1916, the force was in a sorry logistic state. Everything turned on getting all aspects of transportation, and indeed the whole administrative system, put right. It is only possible here to deal with this in bare outline. The river steamer service was built up and re-organized, and, in addition to steamers for carrying troops and stores, a river hospital ship, the *Nabha*, and four paddle steamers and some thirty British Red Cross Society launches were made available for casualty evacuation. All were operated by the Inland Water Transport Division, Royal Engineers. Wharves were made at Basra, and the construction of both metre- and narrow-gauge railway extensions begun. The woefully

Motor transport of 7th Battalion, The North Staffordshire Regiment near Birkandi, Mesopotamia, 1918. The smaller vehicles are Ford Ts used extensively by the British Army in overseas theatres. (IRCT)

understrength animal transport, on which so much had depended until then, was reinforced with an additional two thousand mules and carts. Probably the most important transportation improvement, though, was the large injection of mechanical transport, since this was to have a profound effect on the ultimate success of the operation.

Although animal transport continued to play an essential part in the maintenance of the force, it was the mechanical transport that was now able to provide the real mobility. The ASC made its first appearance in the theatre in January, 1916. A company was sent from Egypt, equipped with 110 Peerless 3-ton lorries, but, although it was involved in part of the operations to relieve Kut, it was a case of too little too late to help improve the logistic situation for that operation. However, it was the start of what was later that year to become a flow of mechanical transport units to the force. Ultimately there were to be forty-two ASC mechanical transport companies, equipped with various types of vehicles, and, in addition, infantry battalions were provided with their own element of MT.

With this influx of mechanical transport came a new type of vehicle, which, although of small load capacity, was able to operate well in the extremes of climate and terrain. This was the Ford van, and some 3,300 were eventually serving in the theatre, proving invaluable both for maintenance of the force and in providing the troop lifts which gave mobility. In addition to the Peerless 3-ton lorry company mentioned above, there was also a company of Packard 3-ton lorries, and these two companies provided the heavier lifting ability. The tactical fast movement of troops by MT became established practice and the combined supply and transport tasks of the ASC and its ability to maintain a force operating in a mobile role confirmed the success of its organization.

By the end of 1916 the overall logistic situation had improved beyond measure and General Maude, who was now Commander-in-Chief, felt able to go on the offensive. From then on all was success, though sadly he was not to live to see victory achieved. His force recaptured Kut on 24 February, 1917, and took Baghdad on 11 March. The force was then being re-supplied by river 500 miles from Basra, water and land transport being completely integrated. When the main advance continued towards Mosul in the autumn, over 500 vehicles were used in the troop-lifting role. When the Armistice was signed, the force had pursued the enemy to Qaiyara, sixty miles short of Mosul under conditions of complete mobility. By this time no one should have doubted the effect that the use of mechanical transport was to have on mobile operations in the future.

Gallipoli *February 1915 – January 1916*

This campaign, undertaken with the French against the Turks, was, as mounted, of doubtful concept and uncertain logistic feasibility. Of the bravery of the soldiers there was no doubt, but it failed in all its aims. It was originally planned as a naval operation and was a piece of bold strategy which deserved success. When this foundered, however, and the concept changed, the subsequent joint amphibious operation lacked the necessary depth of planning and determination by some commanders to carry it through. Little land transport was used since the roads were non-existent, and, indeed, Lord Kitchener himself had decreed that units would sail without their own transport, as the distances were so short, but he was prevailed upon to change his mind. Even so, when it was decided that only animal transport was feasible in the initial phase, there was still the problem of getting it ashore at the right time.

From a transportation point of view, the significance of this campaign is that it was an opposed amphibious operation – the only example in the First World War. The subsequent land battle offered no new insight into transport operations, and there was almost a complete return to

the use of animals. Unlike Mesopotamia, where the introduction of mechanical transport had a profound affect on operations, the tactical situation at Gallipoli offered no such opportunities.

The British Division selected for the assault landing was the last of the Regular Army Divisions, the 29th. With them for the original landings were the Royal Naval Division, the Australian and New Zealand Army Corps (Anzac), and an Indian Brigade, which overall amounted to 60,000 men and 13,000 animals. There were later to be considerable reinforcements. The force assembled in Egypt under the command of General Sir Ian Hamilton. The French contingent, with separate administrative support, had 17,000 men and 3,500 animals.

The established ASC administrative transport of 29th Division consisted of 3-ton lorries, but these were changed for 30-cwt lorries which were considered more suitable for the terrain likely to be encountered. However, indicative of the state of the planning for this campaign was the fact that the Intelligence Branch was unable to advise on roads, and information on the requirement to use animal transport was not given until all the MT re-equipping had been done. In the event the force was almost entirely maintained by animal transport, both pack and carts, throughout the campaign. In addition to ASC, Anzac and Indian drivers, there was also a Zion Mule Corps, formed in Egypt from Palestinian Russian Jews.

The overall operation was mounted from Alexandria. This was an excellent base, but too far from the operation without an advanced base, and two were established at Imbros and at Mudros on the island of Lemnos. These were fifteen and sixty miles respectively from Cape Helles, the landing area. Over the period 24 April to 1 May the whole force was landed over the beaches in the Helles area. On some beaches there were heavy casualties among the troops in the landing boats before they reached the shore, but overall a successful foothold was gained. However, the bridgehead attained was at the best less than two miles deep, and in some areas less than one. There were considerable delays in getting the animal transport ashore and it was not possible to establish the sort of maintenance system to support further advances inland, had, indeed, these been tactically

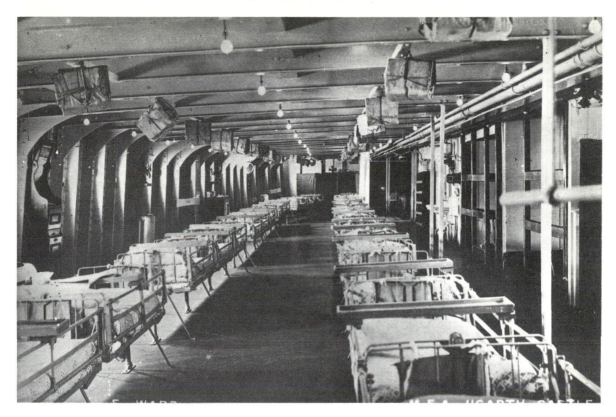

possible. As it was, the overall situation developed into the stagnation of trench warfare in a limited area of formidable terrain with major health hazards, many stemming from the extremes of climate. All the logistics, ranging from casualty evacuation to normal feeding, were excessively difficult, and much had to be carried out under direct enemy fire.

Subsequent reinforcements brought the strength of the force up to twelve divisions by the end of the summer. A further successful landing was made at Suvla, but this was not exploited. However, a base was established there, the only area in which ASC mechanical transport was

used. Some thirty cars, ambulances and 30 cwt lorries were able to operate and the base was developed with the building of jetties and internal roads. The bulk of the administrative transport at Suvla was, however, provided by an Indian mule cart unit with some 2,500 animals.

The shipping used to carry the assault force in this operation was a mixture of RN warships and a variety of troopers. Many were not well suited for the task of an opposed amphibious operation, neither were the boats and barges which they carried for the actual landings on the beaches. All the skill and resolution of the crews of these small boats could not always get them successfully to the shore under the devastating fire that many encountered, and there were severe casualties.

All was not well either before the departure of the force from Alexandria, as there was a muddle over the correct order of stowage of equipment. Some vessels had been incorrectly stowed and departure of the force was delayed while this was sorted out. Neither did all the troopers reach Gallipoli safely. The *Royal Edward*, carrying 1,400 troops, was torpedoed with a considerable loss of

OPPOSITE TOP HMS **Implacable** escorting 2nd Battalion The Royal Fusiliers to 'Y' Beach, Gallipoli, 25 April, 1915. (City of London Headquarters, The Royal Regiment of Fusiliers)

BELOW Wounded coming alongside a hospital ship, Gallipoli, early 1916. (RN Museum, Portsmouth)

ABOVE 'F' Ward of the Hospital Ship HMHS **Garth Castle**, c1915. (RN Museum, Portsmouth)

life. The *Southland*, carrying Australian troops, was also torpedoed, but nearly all the troops and crew were rescued and the vessel was salvaged and reached Mudros.

A number of hospital ships were used in the campaign and had to handle an enormous flood of casualties, both wounded and sick, of which there were 250,000 from the British Empire element. Some well-known liners of the day were converted to provide these hospital ships, among them the *Aquitania*, the *Britannic* and the *Mauretania*. Transporting casualties to these ships was an enormous problem; the sick and wounded travelled in open barges under very unfavourable conditions.

At the end of 1915 the decision was taken to evacuate Gallipoli, and by early January, 1916, this had been successfully completed, 118,000 men, 5,000 animals and 300 guns being conveyed to Egypt, leaving nothing of value behind for the Turks. The campaign added little to the experience of either the operation or the organization of mechanical transport and everyone shared in the failure of the enterprise.

Lords Birdwood and Kitchener in a Sunbeam staff car at Mudros on the island of Lemnos used as a base in support of the Army in Gallipoli. After Kitchener's visit the decision to evacuate Gallipoli was made. (IRCT)

The Balkans and Greece *1915–1918*

This campaign is only covered in broad outline, since no new forms of transport were involved and the operations were not of exceptional significance. However, both the Royal Engineers and the Army Service Corps had to overcome considerable difficulties to provide the successful transportation backing that the force had to have, and for this reason their contribution to the success of the campaign is briefly considered.

The Salonika campaign was a politically motivated 'sideshow', much criticized during its course. It tied up a large force of British and French troops with considerable logistic liabilities, including transportation in all its forms. The operation was mounted in the hope that a confrontation with the Bulgarians would reduce the effectiveness of the German operations on the Western Front by causing them to send troops to their aid. German help to Bulgaria was, in fact, very limited. The policy also involved trying to persuade neutral Greece to side with Serbia and, in so doing, to help rescue that country with the aid of the British and French Forces. In the event, although Bulgaria was contained, and ultimately surrendered at the Armistice, it represented no great strategic victory, since it imposed little strain on Germany, but a victory it certainly was. Maintaining the force over substantial distances of difficult terrain and with wide-ranging, unhealthy climatic conditions, was a considerable feat, not always appreciated. This was achieved in spite of the initial political complexities of operating from Salonika, a base in a neutral country.

The British advance party arrived in Salonika in late September, 1915, and was followed by troops of the 10th Division from Egypt. They arrived in an haphazard order from 5 October, but initially no transport arrived with the infantry battalions. It took until 28 October for the Division to be complete. Already difficulties were occurring with the Greek authorities who requisitioned all available horses and mules which the force had hoped to hire and imposed delays on the

rail movement of a brigade to Doiran, in Serbia. There they were to assist the French, who by then had two divisions in the area. Even after the 10th Division had all arrived, with additional administrative troops, mainly ASC, the force was still largely dependant on animal transport. However, mechanical transport companies of the ASC began to arrive and the maintenance of the troops in the Serbian border area was carried out by a combination of rail, mechanical and animal transport.

By December the weather in the mountainous forward areas had deteriorated considerably, with heavy snow and rain, and the few roads and tracks became morasses. Maintenance became extremely difficult, and to pull the waggons additional mules were required for each team. At this time, also, the capability of further resistance by the Serbian Army was uncertain. The Bulgarian Army mounted a major attack and the British, in danger of being outflanked, carried out a difficult withdrawal back into Greek territory and established a new defensive line north of Salonika. Part of the success of this action was due to the rapid conversion of the animal transport from

Raft evacuating personnel and stores, Gallipoli, January, 1916. (Imperial War Museum)

carts to pack, which enabled stores to be carried more easily along tracks through the mountain passes. The rail line from Doiran was used to capacity during the withdrawal to bring back guns, stores and vehicles and the operation was successfully completed.

Reinforcements in the shape of four more British divisions were by now arriving at Salonika and by the end of February, 1916, there were 120,000 troops and 50,000 animals. This rose to some 180,000 troops and 120,000 animals by the end of the campaign. Each division had some 4,000 mules and a mixed range of 1,000 carts, in addition to the large numbers with the Army and Line of Communication units.

The force remained in the small area round Salonika until May, 1916, when it again took the initiative and advanced to a line between Doiran and the River Struma Valley, in the Seres area, with the French and Serbian forces on the left flank. By the end of the year the force seemed relatively well equipped with mechanical transport, but the communications were long and difficult, with boulder-strewn tracks that were destructive to the vehicles. Furthermore, the Bulgarians had cut the railway in several places, and this increased the necessity for road transport. Some relief was obtained by the use of a Decauville railway which had been built by the French on the left flank of the British, but the road transport was still over-stretched. Sandfly fever and dysentery were prevalent in the transport units and the strain on both drivers and vehicles took its toll. A major contribution by the Royal Engineers towards improving the operating conditions of the transport was the rebuilding of the road from Salonika to Seres.

At this time there were two ASC companies of Albion 3-tonners and four companies of Ford vans. This was increased in 1917 by a further four Ford van companies. Three of these companies were subsequently attached to the Serbian Army, and were with them when, in 1918, the general advance back into Serbia began. Unlike Mesopotamia, however, the force could not achieve the mobility offered by the use of mechanical transport for troop lifting, since all was required in the maintenance role.

Although this was not a campaign that aroused as much interest as either Mesopotamia or Egypt and Palestine, it was nevertheless a considerable test for the new mechanical transport, and for those who operated it. It also confirmed the flexibility of the ASC within its organization, which made a solid contribution to the success of the campaign. The high degree of transportation co-operation between the British, French and Serbian forces was a special feature of the operations; the British had mechanical transport working with both the French and the Serbs, while the French helped with their Decauville railway.

RIGHT *Winter in Serbia, 1915/1916. These Albion 3-tonners were built by the Albion Motor Company of Scotstoun, Glasgow, under the pre war War Office Subsidy Scheme. (IRCT)*

BELOW *Camouflaged mule-drawn ambulance passing ammunition limbers on the Seres Road, Struma, Bulgaria, October, 1916. (IRCT)*

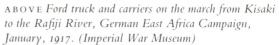

ABOVE *Ford truck and carriers on the march from Kisaki to the Rafiji River, German East Africa Campaign, January, 1917. (Imperial War Museum)*

LEFT *Ford car on railway mounting taking stores from Mingoto to 'C 23', German East Africa, September, 1917. (IRCT)*

BELOW *Canoes and raft carrying Ford truck crossing the Chambesi River, German East Africa, September, 1917. (Imperial War Museum)*

OPPOSITE *Convoy of Crossley trucks with Ford car, German East Africa, September, 1917. (IRCT)*

East Africa 1914–1918

It was not until 1916, when General Smuts took over as Commander-in-Chief of the British force in East Africa, that the Army Service Corps of the British Army became involved with providing and organizing transport in this campaign. Before then it was in the hands of the Indian and South African Armies. But the German Force, under the leadership of the redoubtable Colonel von Lettow-Vorbeck, maintained their mobility in a manner not matched by their opponents, even when the British Army took over. Vorbeck successfully conducted his operations in East Africa for four years and tied up a heterogeneous British Colonial force of a size and at a cost out of all proportion to the size of his own force.

Only a brief mention is made of this campaign, as it introduces no new transport methods to the scene; the operating conditions, however, were in sharp contrast to those in other theatres. The German force, fighting largely in territory of its own colonial administration, and which it knew well in every respect, was able to employ large numbers of native porters. These were very much self-supporting and even carried with them portable boats for river crossings. The British

Colonial force was tied to a more conventional organization and was, initially, politically discouraged from excessive use of the local inhabitants, either as carriers or drivers. But eventually almost a thousand local Africans were trained as mechanical transport drivers and a large number used as carriers.

The force still depended on oxen and mules for much of its transport, and many were lost due to the ravages of the tsetse fly, some 28,000 dying in one operation alone. However, there were eventually twenty ASC mechanical transport companies in the theatre. These included Packard 3-ton lorries and Ford vans, as well as ambulances and cars. There was much debate over selecting the right sort of vehicle for the existing road conditions, and the lighter, smaller vehicles proved less economical. The railways were also used extensively, but were often subjected to guerrilla attack. From a transportation point of view, this campaign extended the use to which mechanical transport could be put, and underlined its capabilities under conditions quite different to those previously experienced by its users, conditions that the British Army was to learn a great deal more about in the future.

Egypt and Palestine *1914–1918*

It is only from late in 1916, when General Murray and his Egyptian Expeditionary Force moved into the Sinai Desert to launch an offensive against the Turks, that the transportation of this force takes on a special significance. At this time there were some 250,000 troops under Murray's command in Egypt. Their primary task was to safeguard the Suez Canal from the Turks, whose main force was in the area of El Arish, on the eastern edge of the Sinai Desert. The logistic preparations for this British offensive were thorough, and although, with one exception, no new technology or modes of transportation were involved, it is the organization and operation thereof that merits examination. In the event, the effectiveness of the whole transportation system made a major contribution to this most successful campaign.

The railways were of prime importance both to the British and to the Turks. Later, the situation of the Turkish railway will be considered briefly, as an example of the effect of resolute guerrilla action against a railway system supplying a force. Firstly, railway construction was undertaken by the Royal Engineers in support of General Murray's operations. It was essential to have a railway to help move the force, and to keep it maintained, across the Sinai Desert. Starting from Qantara, on the eastern edge of the Suez Canal, the laying of a standard gauge track was started in February, 1916. It advanced at the rate of about fifteen miles a month behind the force, until reaching Wadi Ghazze, just short of Ghazi, by which time it was one hundred and forty miles long. In due course

further extensions and branch lines were built. Allowing for the trains involved in the work of construction, this initial line could take seven trains a day carrying troops and stores, and was to provide the bulk of the maintenance movement across the desert when the ultimate advance was made.

Water Point at Shellal, Egypt, 1918. Holt tractor, mules and GS waggon. (IRCT)

BELOW *Water tank train on the El Qantara–Wadi Ghazze railway built and operated by the Royal Engineers across the Sinai Desert, Egypt, 1916. (Museum of Army Transport)*

A new mode of transportation is now introduced – the pipeline. Provision of this was also the task of the Royal Engineers, and in this case the requirement was for water. Ultimately, this essential supply of water for the force was to be piped from a filter plant on the Suez Canal to the area of Gaza and Beersheba. Before the pipeline was completed, water was moved forward by train on the newly constructed railway and distributed to the forward troops by ASC animal transport. In this case camels were used, each carrying 25 gallons. Later, reservoirs and wells were built forward, and ultimately the capture of the wells at Beersheba eased the tenuous but essential and effective pipeline supply.

At this stage in the campaign maintenance of the force forward of the railway was carried out with animal transport, and for this purpose, camels were used, being the most suitable animals for the terrain. The Camel Transport Corps had been formed while the Army in Egypt had been carrying out operations west of the Canal against the Senussi in the Western Desert, prior to the operations with which we are now concerned. The camel requires very careful handling and is more delicate and difficult than its generally

known capabilities would imply. Losses in previous campaigns, such as that in Afghanistan, had been enormous, but now a great effort was made to organize the large numbers involved into properly formed units, providing training, control and real animal management, including hospitalization. The ASC were responsible for camel companies each of 2,000 camels. The camels could carry an average load of 350 pounds, depending on conditions. The ASC also provided the necessary supervisory personnel for the Egyptian drivers. Some 72,000 camels were used during the campaign, and 170,000 Egyptian drivers were employed over the whole period and provided very satisfactory service.

During the winter of 1916 the British Force was twice repulsed by the Turks round Gaza, and, in June, 1917, General Allenby replaced General Murray and reorganized and revitalized the force. During the battles for Gaza a number of changes in the administrative transport took place, and the basic transport introduced was the waggon pulled by four mules. The ASC companies had only

Supply train of the Hejaz railway with Royal Engineer crew, Palestine, 1918. (Museum of Army Transport)

50% of British drivers, the balance being provided from the Anzac contingent, and from the Egyptian Army. In addition to the mule-drawn carts and the camels of the Camel Transport Corps, another animal was introduced into service, the donkey. Two ASC companies, each of 2,000 donkeys, were formed, on the same basis as the Camel Corps, for pack use in the hills. Before General Allenby's successful operations in October, 1917, which broke the Turkish line of Gaza–Beersheba, there were only thirteen ASC mechanical transport companies forward, and all but one was tracked. Eleven of these served the Army Corps heavy artillery. The one wheeled company was a Ford Van Company. Immediately before the action, three 3-ton lorry companies were brought up from Qantara.

Once the Turkish line was broken and the advance towards Jerusalem and Damascus started, the force was maintained by great flexibility and complete co-ordination in the use of its transport. Rail, mechanical and animal transport were all used, while stores were also shipped up by sea and landed across the beaches using surf boats, at Sukerieh, and later at other places up the coast. In December, before Jerusalem was captured, rains slowed down the whole operation and made the roads temporarily impassable to

Camels drawing a GS waggon on the Jaffa–Ludd road, Palestine, 1918. (IRCT)

The Emir Feisal and General MacAndrew, Commander of 5th Division in a Vauxhall staff car, Aleppo, Syria, 1918. (Headquarters Library, Royal Engineers)

MT. However, to replace the MT, camels were used along the coastal sand dunes, even though many sank in the wet sand and were lost; pack animals were used in the Judean Hills. At no time during its advance did the force have to pause because it was not maintained by its transport; it was able to fight and move continuously.

During the advance, work on extending the railways proceeded apace and a bridge was built by the Royal Engineers over the Suez Canal so that the railway to Palestine could be directly linked to the Egyptian railway system and the Army depots and docks which it served. It is appropriate to mention at this stage the work of Colonel T. E. Lawrence with Emir Feisal's Arab force of irregulars. Feisal was the son of Sherif Hussein, self-styled 'King of the Hejaz'. They carried out continuous harassing operations

The first British lorries (Peerless) to enter Damascus, Syria, 1918. (IRCT)

against the Turks, much of which was directed at their transportation. Part of Lawrence's strategy was to carry out hit-and-run raids against the Hejaz Railway, which supplied the Turks and ran the length of Palestine. In so doing, he not only disrupted the Turkish communications, but relieved the pressure on Allenby's right flank. It was an excellent example of the damage that could be exerted on a force by action against the railways supplying it. A further blow against the Turks' transportation was the capture of the port of Aqaba by Lawrence's force. The Hejaz railway was ultimately taken over by Allenby's forces and maintained and operated by the Royal Engineers.

Allenby had to pause in his advance in the spring of 1918, as two British Divisions and twenty-four battalions were sent to the Western Front as a result of the new German offensive and the Indian Army replacements needed time to train and regroup. The final advance, which was to carry the force to Damascus, and on to Aleppo and the defeat of the Turks, started on 19 September, 1918. Although there were still almost 160,000 transport animals involved with the force, now 466,000 strong, at this time mechanical transport was to come into its own. The number of mechanical transport companies ASC had risen to forty, nineteen of which were tracked and drawing the heavy artillery. The wheeled companies contained some 1,600 lorries and

almost 1,500 cars and vans. There were also 530 ambulances.

When Allenby's force broke out from its line east of Jaffa and the three cavalry divisions pursued the enemy, they were maintained by the MT companies following close behind – a considerable achievement. These companies in turn drew their supplies from depots which were established along the coast by ship, or, inland, by rail. Since the cavalry divisions were mounted either on horses or in armoured cars, there was little requirement for troop lifting, if indeed transport in quantity for this task could have been found without prejudicing the maintenance of the force. It was also fortunate that, during the advance, the rain that had hampered the transport before the attack on Jerusalem held off.

During the advance railways to the rear were constantly being improved or repaired by the Royal Engineers, and, in the north, where there had been considerable destruction by the Turks, MT was available to fill the gap until repairs were effected. It was, however, the complete co-ordination of all the transport facilities that enabled the tremendous advance to be supported and victory to be achieved so swiftly.

British Thornycroft and Albion lorries at Constantinople (Istanbul), 1918. Part of the interned Turkish fleet alongside. (IRCT)

North Russia *1918–1919*

General Sir Henry Rawlinson arriving at Archangel, Russia, 11 August, 1919. A Leyland truck in the foreground. (IRCT)

The operations undertaken by the British forces in North Russia were of little significance in the overall war effort, but are included since they introduce a number of new transportation aspects. There were two distinct expeditions sent to North Russia, one destined for Murmansk, and the second for Archangel. Both forces landed initially in the desolate area of Murmansk in June, 1918, the second going on to Archangel in July. The aim of the first small force was to prevent the Kola Inlet from becoming a German submarine base after the defection of Russia. The aim of the second force, which was basically a Military Mission with training instructors and a protection group, was to endeavour to raise and train a new Russian Army from those elements still loyal to the Allied cause. In so doing, it was hoped that the Germans would be compelled to retain an interest in their Eastern front, rather than devoting all to the West.

The two forces remained in Russia after the general Armistice in November, 1918, until September, 1919, and, although training of some Russians recruited to the cause took place, in the end nothing was achieved and all reverted to the Bolsheviks. During this period, however, the forces were involved in relatively minor skirmishes, but had to be maintained, partly under arctic conditions, for distances up to 400 miles from the bases. Some 100,000 locals were also provided with food by the force, with the result that a higher degree of co-operation existed than might otherwise have occurred, but maintenance problems, including transportation, were increased as a result.

Though a single-line railway existed, it could not be depended upon and alternative means of transport had to be made available, the extreme winter conditions requiring a complete reappraisal of the methods of transport. The change from winter to summer conditions brought new problems, when melting snow and ice affected routes and the type of transport that could be used. Carts were built locally to replace sleighs and there was thus no break in the system.

In addition to the British force of two battalions of infantry and two Canadian artillery batteries, there were regiments from France and

OPPOSITE TOP *Horse-drawn sleighs of the ASC in Murmansk, Russia, August, 1919. (IRCT)*

OPPOSITE BELOW *Officers of the British Military Mission in horse-drawn sleigh in front of their headquarters train, Russia, 1919. (Imperial War Museum)*

TOP *British armoured train leaving Medredje Gora, Russia, for the front, 9 September, 1919. (Imperial War Museum)*

CENTRE *Dog-drawn sleighs near Murmansk, 1919. (Imperial War Museum)*

RIGHT *Team of the Reindeer Transport Corps formed to support the British Army in Russia in 1919. Each sleigh could carry about 600 pounds, three reindeer pulling and one in the rear to act as brake, Murmansk, 1919. (Imperial War Museum)*

the United States, and small detachments of Italians and Portuguese. The administrative services included the ASC, who, in their transport role, supervised or operated a wide variety of transport, ranging from mechanical transport to sleighs drawn by horses, reindeer or dogs. They also operated boats on the rivers and lakes. Reindeer sleighs were used extensively in the winter months and, using staging posts, covered distances up to 140 miles from base. About 2,000 reindeer, 500 sleighs, and 1,000 Laplander drivers were employed most successfully.

It is not proposed to dwell on either the small military operations against the Bolsheviks or the administration in detail, but the illustrations do give some idea of what was involved in an area which presented fresh problems and added the requirement for new methods of transport and its control.

In the next chapter we enter the 1920s and another period of stagnation for the Army as a whole. It is not the task of this book to examine the political and military reasons for this situation. Fortunately in the transportation field we are still able to see some advances, which we shall examine.

Ration boat convoy crewed by women leaving for Twda, Russia, 1919. (Imperial War Museum)

5

Between the Wars

THE RUN-DOWN of the Army after the First World War, from its vast wartime establishment to its new peacetime strength, was even more dramatic than that following Waterloo, and the climate of adverse public opinion and financial stringency just as pronounced. The Government was loath to recognize the extent of the military commitment that still existed, even though there were additional colonial or mandated territorial responsibilities, a force to be maintained on the Rhine and the continuing problems of Ireland and India. Financial allocation to the Forces was based on the Government assumption – known as 'The Ten Year Rule' – that the British Empire would not be engaged in any great war in the ten years following 1919. Cuts were the order of the day. Furthermore, there was now an established third arm to the Forces – The Royal Air Force – and the little money that there now was had to be spread even wider, with the result that the Army was starved of funds.

As far as the Army was concerned, it was vital that the process of mechanization should continue in all its forms, from tanks to logistic load carriers. However, replacing the horsed cavalry, quite apart from the financial constraints, was fraught with controversy. It was necessary to agree on what sort of armoured fighting vehicles were needed for the cavalry and the Tank Corps. Furthermore, agreement on the tactical doctrine for their employment, and where this employment was likely to be, was the subject of much political and military debate. All this, to the delight of some and the dismay of others, postponed the demise of the horse in its fighting role.

The further development of suitable mechanical transport to replace outdated wartime vehicles and horses for logistic tasks could not be

Horses to the rescue! A none too successful attempt by a Sunbeam staff car to ford a river, c1920. (Leo Cooper Collection)

considered in isolation. Vehicles had to be capable of reaching the cavalry and infantry in combat, wherever they were, and required a cross-country performance which the wartime vehicles had never achieved. Complete redesigning was essential. As in the case of the cavalry, there was also the sheer cost of providing sufficient numbers of the right sort of vehicles to replace not only the horse, but the obsolescent vehicles as well.

That there was any advance in mechanization under such unfavourable conditions was very much due to the strength of the personalities who emerged as its protagonists and their dedicated but often unpopular efforts to get their views accepted. They grappled with the problems and drove the changes through against all military and political odds. But delays in some areas were inevitable. Two of the Corps most involved with mechanization were the Tank Corps and the Army Service Corps, both of which had received the prefix Royal after the war. The Royal Tank Corps, however, having won its spurs in the war, had a fight on its hands for some time to come; many still needed convincing that the tank should be the main element within the combat arms of a properly balanced mobile force. The RASC was more fortunate, as it ended the war with its role and reputation for the control and management of logistic transport firmly established. This was to help greatly in the drive to enhance and complete its own mechanization.

Although there were extensive operations on the North-West Frontier of India during this period, as well as troubles in Ireland, Palestine and elsewhere, this chapter is not based on campaigns, but is confined to examining the development of mechanical transport on land, and to highlighting new and improved modes of transport by air and sea.

Air Transport

During the War the Royal Flying Corps had successfully devoted its efforts to combat and reconnaissance roles, which fell naturally to it. The newly-formed Royal Air Force was soon to take on the additional task of air transport support for the Army. This was a role that, although developing slowly, was ultimately to provide support of unimagined magnitude. The start was tentative, but nevertheless of considerable importance, since its first cargo was mail, always a vital element in maintaining the morale of the Army.

Many transportation involvements of the

Royal Fusiliers embussing for Belfast in 1922. The vehicle has armour plating to protect driver and passengers. This period of operations in Northern Ireland is not covered in the text. (City of London Headquarters, The Royal Regiment of Fusiliers)

The world's first scheduled airmail service, 17 December, 1918. Run by the Army Postal Service and the Royal Air Force for an experimental period from 17 December, 1918 to 31 August, 1919, between the United Kingdom and Cologne, Germany. The aircraft is a De Haviland DH 9. (Ministry of Defence)

Royal Engineers have already been described, but, in their Army Postal Service role, they were now to be the first administrative users of transportation facilities provided by the Royal Air Force. The question of carrying Army mail by air was first raised in July, 1917, when, due to enemy action, there were heavy losses of mail carried by scheduled ferry service to the BEF. The Royal Flying Corps was at this stage unable to help, due to operational commitments, but after the Armistice an air service was introduced at the instigation of the Royal Engineers (Postal and Courier Service). The experimental service started on 17 December, 1918, and ran until 31 August, 1919, covering the whole area then occupied by the BEF, including the Rhineland. The mail was carried in Handley Page bombers and De Haviland DH9s and, despite some operating problems, was the first successful regular British Postal Air Service. It was to be some time, however, before any unit air moves for the Army occurred.

The first move of an element of an Army unit by air took place on 24 August, 1929, between Cairo and Jerusalem. At that time there was no Army presence in Palestine, internal security having been handed over to the RAF and the Police. Serious rioting between the Arabs and the Jews started at the Wailing Wall in Jerusalem on 23 August and orders were given for an infantry battalion to be sent from the Cairo Brigade to help restore the situation. The 1st Battalion, South Wales Borderers were selected for the task, and two platoons were detailed to be sent by air as immediate reinforcements. Four Vickers Victoria aircraft of 216 Squadron Royal Air Force flew with two platoons of C Company, under the

command of Captain Lochner, from Heliopolis (Cairo) to Kalandia (Jerusalem). They left at 1315 and arrived at 1700, 24 August. One aircraft made a forced landing en route, but was able to continue later the same day. The two platoons were successfully in action immediately after landing and were joined the following day by the remainder of the Battalion, which had travelled by train from Cairo. This was the start of a major Army reinforcement of Palestine, to endeavour to keep the peace between Jew and Arab. It was also to be the start of the tactical, and later strategical, movement of Army units by the Royal Air Force.

The first move by air of a complete infantry battalion did not take place until almost three years later. In June, 1932, the 1st Battalion, Northamptonshire Regiment, commanded by Lieutenant-Colonel T. S. Muirhead, was ordered to move by air from Egypt to Iraq to take over the defensive duties of the Assyrian Levies, who had decided to give up soldiering. At that time a war was taking place between the Iraqi Army and Kurdish insurgents. The move, starting on 22 June, was carried out by nineteen Vickers Victorias, drawn from 6, 70 and 216 Squadrons, Royal Air Force, based in Iraq and Egypt. The distance from Moascar to Hinaidi was 793 miles and the best flight time was 11 hours. Some planes were forced down in the desert by dust storms and others had engine trouble, but the move of fifteen officers and 548 other ranks was successfully completed over six days, including road and rail journeys to company outposts.

The flights were full of minor incidents, and certainly most uncomfortable in the prevailing hot weather. It was evidently made up for, however, by the excellence of the reception that the Battalion received from the RAF on arrival at Hinaidi. The move of infantry battalions by air is now commonplace, but the effect on the local situation then, of the swift arrival of this battalion by air, was understandably impressive.

TOP LEFT *Members of The Northamptonshire Regiment emplaning in a Vickers Victoria at Heliopolis, Egypt, 22 June, 1932, bound for Iraq. (Royal Air Force, Brize Norton)*

LEFT *Members of The Northamptonshire Regiment deplaning from their Vickers Victoria of 216 Squadron Royal Air Force at Hinaidi, Iraq, after an eleven-hour flight of 793 miles from Egypt, 22 June 1932. (Regimental Headquarters, The Northamptonshire Regiment)*

INSET *Lee Enfield rifles (.303) and Lewis guns (.303) secured in the lavatory of a Vickers Victoria aircraft bound for Iraq, 22 June, 1932. (Royal Air Force, Brize Norton)*

H.T. 'LANCASHIRE'

Sea Trooping

Between the two World Wars sea trooping returned very much to the routine of rotating the
infantry battalions, cavalry regiments, artillery
batteries and supporting units that were serving
mainly in India and the Middle East. Trooping
was largely continued in the hands of two famous
lines, the British Indian Steam Navigation Company and Bibby. More than a dozen troopers were
operating during this period. There were some
fifty-three infantry battalions involved and they
were now to travel in considerably greater comfort than previously, though soldiers still slept in
hammocks and fed on folding tables in the same
space as was occupied by the hammocks at night.
It was not until 1936, when BI produced the first
purpose-built troopship, *Dilwara*, of 12,556 tons,
that bunks instead of hammocks were provided,
and these became standard in peacetime. A sister
ship, *Dunera*, was taken into service in 1937.
Soldiers' families now had far better facilities.
They occupied cabins and had their meals in the
third-class dining room, but their husbands still
had to eat and sleep on the troop decks. Warrant
Officers and Sergeants had a Sergeants' Mess, and
those who were married shared cabins with their

The Bibby Line troopship SS **Lancashire**. *The ship
was affiliated to the Royal Corps of Signals. Converted
to a troopship in 1935 she was normally employed in
seasonable trooping to and from India. She had a
distinguished war career, including the Normandy
landings, and was eventually retired in 1956. (Tom
Hartman)*

families and had their meals with them in the
second-class dining room.

P & O, who had been prominent in trooping
until the end of the First World War, did not
manage troopships again until the Second World
War, but their ships became familiar to officers
and their families who could afford to take leave
from India during their six-year tour there, and
sailed home in them at what might be considered
very reasonable prices nowadays – less than the
cost of a cabin on some cross-channel ferries. A
number of troopers were to become very well
known and some vessels in service from early in
this period survived the Second World War and
served on after that war as well. The most famous
ship in this category was the Bibby Line *Lancashire*, which was always a popular ship with soldiers, and was 'adopted' by the Royal Corps of
Signals.

Development of Logistic Mechanized Transport

In 1920 the War Office MT Advisory Board was established as a successor to the MT Committee, which had done much to advance mechanization both before and during the First World War. The time had come to take stock of the experiences of the War and to assess the sort of vehicles that were now needed. The Chairman of the new Board was the head of the RASC, the Director of Supplies and Transport, then Major-General Sir E. E. Carter. He and his Board were responsible for the development of all wheeled vehicles used by the Army, not only technically within the Army, but also in liaison with the civilian motor industry. The Board, to help it in its task, had the experimental workshops of the RASC MT School of Instruction. It was this organization, under the command of Colonel H. Niblett, a civilian professor of mechanical engineering, that was to make such a tremendous contribution to the future of mechanical transport.

Most of the considerable number of load-carrying vehicles remaining at the end of the war were 3–4 ton lorries with solid rubber tyres and were the produce of the pre-war subsidy scheme, described in Chapter 3. The continuation of such a scheme was essential if sufficient of the right sort of vehicles were to be made available for any operations in the future, without prohibitive expenditure on stockpiling. However, it was clear that the new range of vehicles had to have a cross-country performance, which the war-time vehicles had lacked. To meet this essential requirement, and at the same time provide a viable commercial vehicle within the subsidy scheme, was a major problem.

There were strong pleas from some for tracked vehicles. Sensibly, these were discarded as an overall solution, as they did not meet the criteria of commercial viability, but some half-tracks were subsequently introduced as specialist vehicles. By 1923, however, a compromise solution had been found. The vehicle produced had only a 30 cwt carrying capacity, but had pneumatic tyres, which, with its light weight, gave it a creditable cross-country performance. More important, it was acceptable to a number of motor manufacturers, despite their initial misgivings about pneumatic tyres, which they still regarded as luxurious. By 1926 there was the required quota of one thousand of these vehicles

A French Latil logging tractor under trials as a recovery vehicle for the RASC, c1923. (IRCT)

in civilian use, which could be used as necessary by an expeditionary force. The acceptance of pneumatic tyres was hailed as a great advance and another important stage in the development of MT had been reached.

The technical problems of providing a cross-country performance with greater carrying capacity still remained, however. A 30 cwt vehicle was clearly too small, with only the load capacity of the horse-drawn GS waggon. Compared with the old 3-ton vehicle, it was uneconomical because of the additional numbers of vehicles and drivers that would be required to carry the same overall quantities. The design of a six-wheeler vehicle proved to be the answer. In 1922 the RASC Experimental Workshop, in conjunction with the Morris and Thornycroft motor companies, developed a 30 cwt light version for cavalry and infantry unit administrative vehicles and a 3-ton model for RASC Divisional units. The first trials of these vehicles on military manoeuvres took place in 1926, by which time a number of manufacturers had entered the subsidy scheme. By the end of that year these vehicles were in full commercial production; an overseas market had been created, and they were sold in many countries where their superior cross-country performance proved invaluable.

Lord Montagu of Beaulieu, who had been adviser on mechanical transport services to the Government of India from 1915 to 1919, carried out a trial with the Thornycroft 6-wheeled lorry in 1927, on an expedition which he undertook from Beirut to Baghdad. He reported that the vehicle gave a very satisfactory performance across the desert. Previously, during the time of his appointment in India, Lord Montagu, as a pioneer motorist before the war, was a great advocate of mechanization in the Indian Army. He had been instrumental in making the direct purchase of the Ford vans from the United States in the First World War. These were the first vehicles with any sort of cross-country performance in the war, and, as related in the last chapter, were sent to Mesopotamia in 1916 and were widely used elsewhere. These vehicles, too, were among the first to be used on the North-West Frontier in 1919. However, the new six-wheelers which he tested were a different proposition,

having been specifically designed for the task.

In 1927 38 (MT) Company RASC was formed in Aldershot and equipped with sixty 30 cwt Morris six-wheelers. They then went via Hong Kong with 15 Brigade to form part of the Shanghai Emergency Force. In Hong Kong they successfully carried out extensive trials with their six-wheelers, including hill-climbing and the crossing of water obstacles. So it was that a new range of Army six-wheeled vehicles, in a light, medium and heavy form, had been developed, tested and accepted into service at this time. The Army now also led the way with the use of pneumatic tyres. They were on all its new vehicles, and special balloon tyres for use in the desert were already under development in conjunction with the Dunlop Rubber Company. Almost as important, though, was the co-operation that was built up between the RASC Experimental Workshop and the motor and tyre manufacturers. This was to be of the utmost value to Army transportation when the time came for further development and expansion, with the technical training of officers undertaken by the manufacturers.

In 1928 an important change in the organization of the development and provisioning of Army mechanical transport took place. The responsibility for these matters at the War Office passed from the Quartermaster-General to the Master-General of the Ordnance, and the basic effect was that the RASC were no longer responsible for the research, design and manufacture of vehicles; these duties passed to the Royal Army Ordnance Corps. They did, however, continue to remain responsible for the inspection, storage, issue and repair of all RASC vehicles, including those for medical units. They also retained responsibility for the impressment and subsidizing of commercial vehicles, which ensured that, when mobilization took place, sufficient vehicles were immediately available. An RASC organization was set up within the UK to list and inspect vehicles and control the scheme. In the event, in 1939, some 14,000 vehicles were able to be impressed immediately and a parallel scheme for hiring was smoothly implemented.

By 1934 great advances had been made in the design and efficiency of the normal four-wheeled vehicle in the 3-ton range, and they now met most of the requirements for the Army's normal tasks. This was even so in the desert, when fitted with the newly developed tyres. It was therefore decided that the six-wheeler which had proved so successful as the standard Army load carrier, but was more expensive, should only be used in units where their greater mobility was essential. When war came again in 1939 the logistic transport of the Army was in a better stage of development and implementation than anyone who had not been concerned with the fight for success had a right to expect.

The Reduction in Horse Transport

By 1921, when the peacetime establishment of the RASC transport units had been settled, there were still thirty-one horse transport companies left. These were equipped with the GS waggon, and there had been four hundred and five companies so equipped during the war, in addition to the vast number of different sorts of animal units, both pack and draught, which were disbanded at the end of the war. Mechanization, within the constraints outlined above, was, however, proceeding inexorably, and, with the advent of suitable cross-country vehicles, the RASC horse transport companies were gradually disbanded.

The last of the companies, 4 (HT) Company, ended its days at Catterick on 31 December, 1929. With its going an era had ended, though there still remained some elements of unit horse transport in infantry and cavalry units and in the Territorial Army, which were also replaced with mechanical transport before 1939. The age of horse transport was not yet dead, however, and it was indeed fortunate that the animal transport skills were kept alive at the RASC Training Centre at Aldershot, where a training company was retained, since animal transport in pack form was to return in strength in the Second World War.

In India, however, where a large part of the British Army was still serving at the beginning of the Second World War, some animal transport still featured as logistic transport until that time, and expanded enormously thereafter. However, even on the North-West Frontier, where animal

THIS PAGE AND THE FOLLOWING TWO PAGES
A selection of vehicles developed between the wars, some of them under the War Office Subsidy Scheme which was reintroduced soon after the war. (Leo Cooper Collection)

1 ton Morris Roadless, 1925

1 ton Morris Roadless carrier, 1925

15 cwt Crossley-Kegrisse, 1926

Morris light six-wheeled lorry, 1928

Leyland lorry with Carden-Loyd on recovery trailer, 1932

Austin light car, 1928

Leyland lorry with Carden-Loyd entering on ramps

Morris light six-wheeled staff car, 1928

Leyland medium six-wheeled F.C. drive lorry, 1932

Crossley light six-wheeled staff car, 1929

Morris D-type with ambulance body

30 cwt Morris CD Model, 1936

Triumph solo, 1927

Morris D-type as desert staff car

Douglas solo, 1931

Albion, Thornycroft and Guy four-wheeled lorries

Matchless 350cc, c 1935

Thornycroft six-wheeler, widely used in the desert

BSA 500cc M20 twin, c 1938

transport had predominated for so long, mechanical transport began to appear, and when the Third Afghan War started in May, 1919, a number of MT companies of the RASC were involved. Later, between 1921 and 1924, when there were major operations in Waziristan, there was a further reduction in animal transport in these operations, as roads were built by the Sappers and MT was able to operate. The RASC were to remain in India until 1928, when their responsibilities were handed over to the Indian Army Service Corps which had been formed in 1923 from the Indian Supply and Transport Corps. The RASC had not only been widely engaged with their MT companies on the North-West Frontier operations, where many of the companies had an Indian element, but also left behind in India a major contribution to the mechanization of the Indian Army. Almost 20% of all ranks of the RASC transferred to the IASC and helped to establish the new Corps on a sound mechanical footing.

Ropeways and Railways – India

When major operations started on the North-West Frontier in 1919, improvements to the transportation facilities were sought since the roads were very limited. The first project was to build a unique ropeway to convey stores from Jamrud in the Peshawar Valley to Landi Khana on the Afghanistan Frontier, a distance of some twenty miles, following the line of the Khyber Pass. This project, the building of which was initially supervised by an officer of the Royal Engineers, was completed by the Mechanical Transport Department in India and operated by the RASC. The ropeway was built in six sections, and the steel cables were suspended from standards at varying distances and heights along the route which rose to over 3,700 feet. The system worked on the basis of endless cables driven by engines between each section, from which carriers capable of taking 3 cwt of stores were suspended. The ropeway was completed in 1920 and for six years was used

Camel convoy in the Khyber Pass, Third Afghan War, 1920. (National Army Museum)

effectively for supplying the military camps be-tween Jamrud and Landi Khana. The tribesmen made few attacks on this system, but it was not used at night and arms and ammunition were not sent by this means to avoid placing temptation their way. The only other form of ropeway used for Army transportation was the Teleferica Rope-way used by 14 British Army Corps in Italy in 1917, but this utilized a fixed cable and the load was winched.

A construction of greater magnitude, and still existing, was the Khyber Railway, built through the Khyber Pass between Jamrud and Landi Khana, and opened in 1925. There had been con-siderable pressure to extend the existing railway from Jamrud through the Khyber, to improve the logistic situation of the forts there and to mini-mize the protection requirements of troops and stores through the Pass. It had earlier been sug-gested that it was too difficult, but in 1920 the Royal Engineers undertook the planning and su-pervision of the extension. It was a considerable engineering feat and took five years to complete. The extension involved complex alignments that were ingeniously devised over a zigzag route, using reversing stations. Two high viaducts were also constructed and the stations were all in pro-tected areas. Though constructed too late to assist in the Third Afghan War, it was to be invaluable in helping to maintain the *status quo* in the Khyber.

With the growing realization among many in Britain that war with Germany was inevitable, re-armament was creeping in. A number of alarms and excursions in the Far and Middle East took place in the last few years of the period prior to the outbreak of the Second World War in 1939. The opportunity was taken to thoroughly test the new range of logistic vehicles and to revise trans-port control organizations to take account of the greater mobility and changing tactical doctrines that were now appearing in divisions as a result of mechanization. In Egypt, for example, after the Munich Crisis, the 7th Armoured Division was formed from the Mobile Division and a new concept for the operation of the logistic transport within the Division was evolved which was to stand it in good stead in the approaching war. Overall, mechanization was by no means com-plete, neither were all the vehicles perfect for the job, or in sufficient numbers. Nevertheless, de-spite the financial stringency that had existed, a great deal had been achieved by 1939. But, even at this stage, the horse was about to re-assert its usefulness to the Army's transportation needs. An encore indeed!

Baggage train out on column, North-West Frontier, 17 April, 1936. Mechanical transport is now included. (Leo Cooper Collection)

6

The Second World War

IN KEEPING with the trend of the Army's main preparations, the state of transport resources at the beginning of the Second World War was, relatively, not as advanced as it had been in 1914. This overall situation did not exist through any lack of endeavour among many enlightened and dedicated officers, and, exceptionally, some resolute politicians. It was simply that, until the German occupation of the Slovakia Sudetenland after Munich, there was not the overall political will, nor the money, to prepare for the inevitable war. By then it was almost too late. So, in 1939, the British Army was just not equipped to fight the Germans. Amid the deficiencies, they lacked the sort, and, more important, the quantity of transportation support that was required against an enemy that had devoted so much time, thought and practice towards producing the means of winning a modern mobile war.

It was a war during which there were tremendous changes in the methods of transportation. Technical innovations greatly improved, and added to, the available range and performance of vehicles to meet every requirement. These were ultimately manufactured in vast quantities. Specialized vessels of every shape and size, with harbouring facilities to match, were produced to meet needs ranging from river crossings to assault landings from the sea. The air was to become a standard means of delivering both personnel and stores, but often at the receiving end of aerial stores delivery animal transport was to be found as the ground link, still very much

alive and kicking! All this, though, was to take time, and the depressing transportation inadequacies of the first two years of the war still had to be overcome.

Only five campaigns – the BEF 1939–1940, North Africa, Italy, Burma and North-West Europe – are included in the text, since they cover most types of transport used in the War, and the differing conditions of their operation. Similarly, only sufficient tactical background to each campaign is given to show the requirement and effect of transportation on the campaign. The wide coverage of illustrations gives some indication of both the range and tasks of transport wherever the Army was serving.

The British Expeditionary Force *1939–1940*

The BEF moved to France over three weeks and this was completed by 7 October, 1939. Some 170,000 troops and their equipment, with 20,000 vehicles, crossed the Channel without enemy opposition and landed through the ports of Normandy and Brittany. There were four divisions, and Corps and Army troops, and each had their slice of logistic transport, the bulk of which was provided by the RASC. For the first time the RASC was to take the field as a completely mechanized corps, but the provision of vehicles to enable this to take place was not an easy matter. It is worth dwelling on this situation a little to gain

British Expeditionary Force (BEF) landing in France, 1940. This contingent includes members of The Royal Warwickshire Regiment, The East Yorkshire Regiment and The Green Howards. (Leo Cooper Collection)

an idea of the extent of the logistic transport problem at the start of the War. The four divisions, together with the Army and Corps troops, were assigned sixty-two RASC MT Companies. However, before the War, the twelve companies for the divisions, organized on a commodity basis, (i.e., each company basically carried either ammunition, petrol or supplies) were only in cadre form, and all the remaining companies had to be found by mobilizing peacetime units engaged in routine transport duties.

The bulk of the vehicles for all these units had to be obtained on mobilization by the impressment scheme, described in the last chapter, and there were very few new vehicles. The number of vehicles actually held by units in peacetime was very small indeed, and all the purpose-built six-wheelers had to be converted to ambulances and workshop vehicles. In the event, the impressment scheme worked very well, and in a few days some 14,000 vehicles were gathered in from civilian operators, checked, repainted and issued to the newly mobilizing units. Without them the BEF could not have gone to war.

In France transport was in very short supply, partly due to the long lines of communication from the western ports, from where, initially, all maintenance for the force had to come. These ports had been selected to disperse stocks against the likelihood of air attack. It was planned to use the French railways (SNCF) to move forward supplies, but overloading of the system and enemy action was greatly to reduce its effectiveness. Although the Royal Engineers were involved in the operation of SNCF, their role, initially, was limited by the French. It was not until the campaign really started in May, 1940, that they were able to take over more control and maintain running under what were by then extremely difficult conditions.

To reinforce the overstretched RASC transport, four Indian Mule Companies of the Royal Indian Army Service Corps (RIASC) were

LEFT *One of the 'Small Ships'. A trawler loaded with troops leaving Dunkirk, May, 1940. (Imperial War Museum)*

CENTRE *A fully laden destroyer arriving at Dover with men of the BEF evacuated from Dunkirk, 26 May, 1940. (Royal Naval Museum)*

BOTTOM *The end of the liner **Lancastria**, sunk off St Nazaire, as seen from a rescue boat, 17 June, 1940. Hundreds of men are swimming away from the liner. Of the 5,800 known to have embarked 3,000 perished, but the figures are thought to have been higher. (Imperial War Museum)*

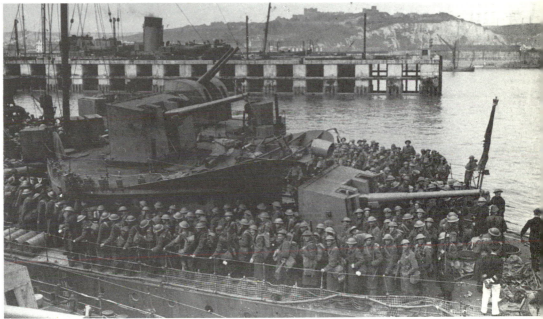

Men of 61st Division at boat drill on the SS **Oronsay** *en route to Norway, 1940. The introduction of British troops to Norway in an attempt to stem the German advance failed and the force was evacuated in June, 1941. This campaign is not covered in the text. (Imperial War Museum)*

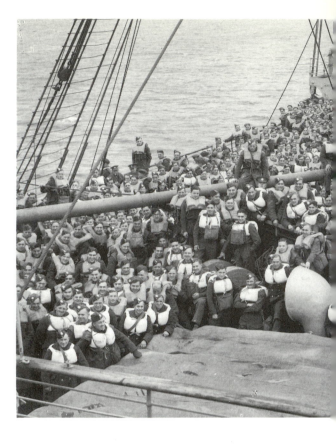

Landing Craft Assault (LCA) leaving the mother ship for the beach with Commandos embarked, Vaagso, Norway. This successful Combined Operations raid, supported by the Royal Navy, took place on 27 December, 1941. Not covered in text. (Imperial War Museum)

brought in, complete with their mules and wag-gons, and these were the first Indian Army Troops on operations in the War. In addition, a Cypriot-manned RASC Mule Company was em-ployed, the first of a number to be used later in other theatres. Together, these provided the only animal transport used by the British Army in France. The German Army by comparison, de-spite their high degree of mechanization, used many more horses in 1939, on logistic tasks. Their ninety infantry divisions each had 4,800 horses, some with as many as 6,000. Throughout the war the Germans used 2.7 million horses.

The German *Blitzkrieg* started on 10 May, 1940, with the invasion of Holland, Belgium and Luxembourg. By 21 May the German out-flanking movement, sweeping towards the Chan-nel, had cut the main rail supply link to the south at Abbeville. The maintenance lifeline of the BEF had been severed, and from then on it was only a matter of time before the Force ran out of all its requirements for survival. Evacuation of the Force, mainly from Dunkirk and Cherbourg, was

implemented. Admiral Ramsay organized the evacuation fleet of every sort of small boat and ship, and attention was turned from land trans-port and its destruction to sea transport and life-saving. Some 340,000 British, French and Allied soldiers were evacuated, but all their equipment was lost. Both the larger transports and the smaller boats were constantly attacked from the air and damage and casualties were significant. A frightful incident was the sinking of the 20,000-ton liner *Lancastria* off St Nazaire with great loss of life. Probably the last significant troop-carrying transport move in the campaign was that by 226 Company RASC, who carried 157 Brigade 200 miles in their withdrawal to Cher-bourg and evacuation on the last troopship to sail on 18 June.

The re-equipping of the Army on its return from France as far as vehicles were concerned was helped by a further drawing-in of vehicles under the impressment scheme. The total was increased to 35,000 of which the original 14,000 had been lost. After that it was a matter of patience, with the motor manufacturers struggling to make up the deficiencies. The build-up started slowly, but, with the help of imported American vehicles, particularly for the Middle East and India, stocks were replaced, many new models being improve-ments on the originals. RASC drivers employed with MT units based in the UK were released for service overseas by employing members of the Women's Service, the Auxiliary Territorial Ser-vice (ATS, now Women's Royal Army Corps) as drivers in these home service units. While some units were mixed and had both RASC and ATS drivers, others became completely composed of ATS, and they drove everything from staff cars to load-carrying vehicles. Many of the officers in these MT units were found from members of the FANY and Women's Legion, whose predecessors had served in France in the First World War.

OVERLEAF *Members of the Auxiliary Territorial Service (ATS), FANY, at a meal halt in the United Kingdom, September, 1941. The ATS performed tasks of almost every description in order to relieve their male counterparts for service in the forward areas and they served in nearly every overseas theatre of operations. (Imperial War Museum)*

TOP *Cypriot pack mule company on the coast road, Syria, July, 1940 during operations in the Eastern Mediterranean. These operations are not covered in the text. (Leo Cooper Collection)*

ABOVE *Army stores being loaded onto a Royal Navy cruiser during the ill-fated operations to support Greece, November, 1940. (Imperial War Museum)*

North Africa

With Italy entering the War in June, 1940, North Africa and the Italian colonies became the next focal point, and General Wavell, the Commander-in-Chief, Middle East, had plenty on his hands, but his force had considerable success in Eritrea and Abyssinia. Elsewhere was more difficult. General O'Connor's Western Desert Force, with the 7th Armoured Division and the 4th Indian Division, and later the 6th Australian Division, made spectacular advances into Cyrenaica and Libya in the period up until February, 1941. They were unable to exploit these successes, however, as there was insufficient transport to maintain the force at the distance of 500 miles that it had advanced from its bases. They were indeed fortunate that they had as much transport as they did, and this was due to the foresight of the War Office in 1939, before the

War started, in having stockpiled in Egypt 500 GMC Bedford lorries. Nevertheless, O'Connor's force, with never more than two divisions, had destroyed an Italian force of ten divisions. His success, though, had drawn the German Army into North Africa, in the shape of General Rommel's Afrika Corps, and for the next two years the desert battle ebbed and flowed. Finally, the situation was stabilised in early 1942, after Tobruk had fallen to the Afrika Corps and the British Forces had suffered a damaging retreat. General Auchinleck took over command and established a defensive position along the El Alamein line.

In October, 1942, the Eighth Army, as it now was, and under the command of General

Highland Light Infantry in Bedford QL 3-ton trucks and Carriers, universal (Bren carriers). Western Desert, June, 1942. (Leo Cooper Collection)

Bedford OY 3-ton trucks being unloaded from a battleship of the Royal Navy, Algeria, 1943. (Imperial War Museum)

Montgomery, fought the successful Battle of El Alamein, to start the ultimate defeat of Rommel's Afrika Corps. At this time an Anglo-American force under General Eisenhower was landing in French North Africa and the two Armies were to link up in Tunis in May, 1943, having together defeated the German and Italian Armies in North Africa. In the three years that had elapsed since the campaign started in North Africa, the transportation scene had changed dramatically. This was essentially a war of movement, and, without adequate transport and overall logistic support, the cause of failure earlier in the campaign, the armour could not have exploited its successes.

Desert driving conditions required special techniques, and the wear and tear on both drivers and vehicles could be enormous, especially when the daily distances covered increased. But the new range of vehicles now appearing stood up well to the conditions, when properly handled and serviced methodically. Their effectiveness was only matched by the tremendous response of the drivers to the tasks with which they were faced. In 1940 4,000 Chevrolet vehicles directed from the United States had been received by RASC units.

In 1941 the demand was for 14,000, though the unsuccessful campaign in Greece creamed off some of these replacements and there were heavy losses there. The requirement for vehicles was so large that, by June, 1941, an assembly plant had been established in Suez, so that space on the valuable shipping could be saved by sending American vehicles cased and 'fully knocked down'. By the time of the Battle of El Alamein some 45,000 vehicles had passed through the plant and the losses sustained at the fall of Tobruk in June, 1942, and the retreat to the El Alamein line had been made up.

The logistic transport tasks were widely varying and each presented their own particular problems. They are typified by the following examples. RASC troop-carrying vehicles for the infantry were now standard and an essential requirement in any pursuit of the enemy in the desert, to keep up with the armour. These were based on standard 3-ton lorries, but the numbers

A railcar used as an ambulance train, Algeria, 1943.
(Museum of Army Transport)

now involved had greatly increased. 10-ton lorries were, however, a new range of vehicles and
were used on L of C routes where there was a
reasonable road, as off the road they tended to bog
down in sand. They did, however, reduce the
overall number of vehicles required, and therefore
the number of drivers, of whom there was an
acute shortage.

The carriage of the enormous quantity of petrol required, mostly in the standard 3-ton vehicle,
was expensive in transport as the Army was still
largely dependent throughout the campaign on
the four-gallon 'flimsy' can, which was very
wasteful because of leakage. Losses from this
cause could be as high as 30% across bad terrain,
and could also be distinctly dangerous. Water,
too, presented problems in the desert and required
much transport for its distribution, even with the

water ration down to as little as half a gallon per man per day, which it often was. There were few specialist water tankers initially, and improvisation, both in vehicle types and suitable containers, was necessary for most of the campaign. The Royal Engineers repaired wells and cisterns and laid pipelines under most difficult conditions, but the water still had then to be carried forward in vehicles for distribution to units.

An entirely new vehicle in the campaign was the tank transporter, and the famous Diamond T made its appearance. This vehicle was designed for the out-of-battle movement of tanks to avoid track wear, and for the recovery of damaged or broken-down tanks from the battlefield. Although treated as something of a novelty early in the campaign, they were more than to prove their worth and were to become an increasingly important element of RASC transport as the War progressed.

Evacuation under fire. A Matilda tank being evacuated by a Diamond T tank transporter, Western Desert, 1942. (Imperial War Museum)

Mention must be made of all the different nationalities that provided drivers for the logistic transport under the control of the RASC in this campaign. In the early days Cypriots, for both AT and MT, were enlisted, and these were followed by Maltese and Palestinian Jews, all of whom were involved in operations in the desert. Mauritians, Sudanese and Singalese were also in operational companies and were joined by the Dominion Forces of Australia and New Zealand, and many companies, both MT and AT, were provided by the RIASC. The South African force also supplied units, and, in the Base, Palestinian Arabs were formed into units with British cadres. By the time of the El Alamein offensive, in addition to the integral divisional RASC companies, there was RASC transport support equivalent to sixty-three 3-ton companies for the subsequent advance to Tripoli. These were still only barely sufficient for the enormous quantities of ammunition, petrol and supplies that had to be carried forward continuously in support of the mobility now achieved by the armoured force.

Two major changes in organizations affecting transport occurred in 1942. Firstly the Corps of Royal Electrical and Mechanical Engineers (REME) was formed and became responsible for the repair of all Army equipment. The RASC Companies retained their unit vehicle workshops, but all the personnel became REME. Secondly, the RAOC took over the responsibility for the storage and issue of RASC vehicles. This responsibility the RASC had retained for their own vehicles after the RAOC took over the Army's vehicle research and procurement responsibilities from them in 1928. Although the RASC now lost a degree of control over the issue and repair of its own vehicles, and had some misgivings, this was clearly a realistic and sensible re-organization in line with mechanization. It was to work extremely effectively.

During the campaign animal transport was revived in great numbers, but initially was used mainly in the base areas where it replaced the hard-pressed mechanical transport. It was not to be long, however, before AT Pack Units were to be back in the thick of things after the landings in Algiers, and both the RASC and RIASC operated AT Companies there. Indeed, before this they

were already being used in the successful campaigns in Eritrea and Abyssinia.

The Western Desert Railway played an important part in the logistic support of the force, and the move forward of troops from the Canal Zone. At the beginning of the War it ran from Alexandria to Mersa Matruh, and plans were made for its extension. Water supply was a major problem in the desert as the engines were then steam, and a water pipeline had to be laid as well as the track. Water was also carried forward by rail in tankers. By June, 1942, the line, laid mainly by the New Zealand Railway Construction Group, had reached Belhamed, a few miles east of Tobruk. The line required extensive repair after the retreat to El Alamein and the subsequent advance, but was quickly reopened, and diesel engines, now obtained, reduced the water requirement.

Italy

Following the successful conclusion of the North African campaign, the Anglo-American force turned its attention to Italy. The first step was the invasion of Sicily on 10 July, 1943. This was the largest amphibious operation to date, and an impressive fleet of amphibious craft was used in the assault by General Patton's 7th US and Montgomery's 8th Armies. Gliders of the 1st Airborne Division were also used, not totally successfully, for the first time. Following the conquest of Sicily, the assault across the Straits of Messina was made on 3 September. Although the Italians quickly capitulated, the force was to meet much stronger opposition from the Germans.

A new vehicle is now introduced, the American amphibious DUKW, which carried 2½ tons.

Landing Craft Tank (LCT) and Landing Craft Infantry (LCI) waiting to be signalled ashore, Sicily, 10 July, 1943. (Leo Cooper Collection)

Four amphibious companies of the RASC, equipped with these vehicles, maintained the 5th British and 1st Canadian Divisions across the Straits from Messina to beaches just north of Reggio. The DUKWs and landing craft were also used to ferry troops and maintenance stores up the coast to avoid road obstructions. The DUKWs were to prove invaluable throughout the campaign and were used extensively to cross water obstacles before bridges were repaired, and for maintenance by sea.

Animal transport was introduced into the campaign from the very beginning, and was to form an essential part of the logistic transportation.

Initially, two troops of pack mules accompanied the leading brigade of 5th Division into the hill country behind Reggio, having landed with them. The mules did not take too kindly to the crossing in an LCA, but they stayed with the brigade for the next five months.

Two further sea landings were made by the British and American Forces, in the early stages of the campaign. The first, at Taranto, by elements of the 1st Airborne Division, carried by ships of the Royal Navy, was unopposed, but that at Salerno on 9 September met stiff opposition. The two Armies, the Eighth Army to the east and the Fifth Army to the west, then began their advance north. The Germans had destroyed the docks and all tunnels, rail and road bridges, down to the last culvert, when they withdrew. The Royal Engineers had an enormous repair problem, while the transport necessary to carry the materials had to be found by the RASC – a very large bill. A variety of transport was used for the task, the RASC carrying the bridging equipment on

specialist vehicles and providing tippers and other load carriers. There was the very closest co-operation between the two Corps mutually concerned with transportation.

In the meantime the force had to be maintained, using all possible means. The railway line north of Bari could not be repaired to keep pace with the advance, but in the west the line was working from Naples to Arezzo. RASC water transport companies were now introduced into the campaign, and four companies operating 131 vessels were used to carry supplies along the coast. They carried 200,000 tons in 12 months.

The pack transport companies were eventually using 45,000 mules and horses in the forward mountainous areas. It took two companies to maintain a brigade up to 10 miles from a road-

General B. L. Montgomery, Commander 8th Army, in a DUKW of 51st (Highland) Division, Sicily, July, 1943. The initials DUKW have no significance other than the maker's identification. (Leo Cooper Collection)

*The ubiquitous Jeep. A Willys/Ford Truck ¼ ton 4 × 4
(four-wheel drive) first used as a logistic vehicle in the
British Army during the campaign in Italy. (IRCT)*

*Mules returning from a forward delivery being led past
a blazing petrol supply truck hit by straffing enemy aircraft
a few minutes earlier, Italy, 1943. (IRCT)*

head. In most cases this was a Jeephead, the 'terminus' for another vehicle introduced into the RASC range of logistic vehicles at this time – the American Jeep – one of the most versatile vehicles to be produced in the War. The American 5th Army was well equipped with them, and eventually the RASC in the three British divisions in 5th Army were equipped with platoons of Jeeps with 10 cwt trailers. Without them and the pack mules many of the operations in the campaign would have been unsustainable. One supplemented the other. When the Jeeps could go no further, the pack animals took over. The Jeeps and trailers were particularly useful in taking artillery ammunition to gun positions in the hills; during the battle for Cassino, a whole division was maintained by them.

The two Allied Armies advanced up central

BELOW *Guards embarking in the* **Derbyshire** *in Naples docks for the landing at Anzio, 17 January, 1944. The ship was originally built in 1935 but was later converted to a LSI along with many other vessels of similar size. (Leo Cooper Collection)*

LEFT *Vehicles and troops on the upper deck of an LST in convoy approaching Anzio, January 1944. (Leo Cooper Collection)*

CENTRE *A section of RASC bridging vehicles of 78th Division in Italy during the winter of 1943/1944. (IRCT)*

BOTTOM *Mule convoy crossing the River Ronco, Italy, 1944. (IRCT)*

RIGHT *A caique of the Special Boat Service (SBS) during operations in the Aegean, 1943. (Imperial War Museum)*

CENTRE *Loading stripped-down 40mm Anti Aircraft (AA) guns on the casing of the submarine HMS **Rorqual** (Lieutenant-Commander L. W. Napier RN) at Beirut, Lebanon, 20 October, 1943, destined for Leros, Dodecanese Islands. There was great difficulty in running supplies to the remaining British garrison in the face of enemy action until the Germans were finally cleared from the Aegean. (Royal Naval Submarine Museum, Gosport, Hampshire)*

BOTTOM *Ferry pontoon approaching the left bank landing on the River Tigris, Baghdad, Iraq, June, 1944. (Colonel Frank Jagger, late Royal Engineers)*

Italy towards Rome and Florence, slowly and painfully overcoming the strong German opposition. The terrain provided natural obstacles which aided the Germans in their defence, and they reacted strongly to any attempt to bypass them. The bloody battle for Cassino and the determined containment on the Anzio beachhead were examples. It was not until June, 1944, that Rome was reached. The overall logistics of the campaign were made extremely difficult by lack of communications, either because they had been destroyed or were non-existent. Transportation in all its aspects had to react swiftly to rapid changes brought about by these factors, and improvisation was a constant necessity. With a combination of different types of transport, its use planned and operated with great skill and resolution, the essential support was produced throughout.

Before leaving this campaign, which was to continue until the ultimate defeat of the Germans in North West Europe, one further new type of transportation used in its last phase requires mentioning. This is the American tracked, lightly armoured amphibious vehicle – LVT, which was introduced into the RASC. A regiment, consisting of a headquarters and five squadrons was formed in April 1945. It was used in the assault role, and could carry a brigade HQ and three infantry battalions together with sixteen 25pdr guns, and Royal Engineer assault squadron. The Regiment operated very successfully in a series of assaults in the area of the Po Valley and Lake Comacchio. The RASC personnel also manned storm-boats in the same type of operations in the area.

During the whole period of the land operations in the Mediterranean area, the Royal Navy, with its main forces involved in amphibious operations and keeping the supply routes open, was also acting in close support of the army using a less usual form of sea transportation for the purpose, the submarine. From 1941 onwards, submarines of the Alexandria Flotilla were used to carry Commando raiding parties in attacks against a variety of targets including the railways on the Adriatic coast of Italy. HMS *Truant* – Commander H. C. V. Haggard in command – was one such vessel involved in these operations. Later, submarines operating from both Alexandria and Beirut, carried supplies and personnel

to Malta, then under siege. In September, 1943, Leros in the Dodecanese Islands, taken on the surrender of Italy was also reinforced by submarine – HMS *Rorqual* – Commander L. Napier in command. As the illustration for this incident shows, the guns and vehicles involved were unusually carried on the casing of the submarine.

Burma

With the fall of Singapore in February, 1942, the Japanese turned their attention to Burma. From there they hoped to move into India, also to cut the Burma road, and with it the help that was being given to Chiang Kai-shek in China. The British Forces in Burma – The Burma Army – was weak, consisting of two incomplete divisions. Although these were later to be joined by the American General Stilwell's Chinese force from Chiang Kai-shek's army in north Burma, they were together insufficient to stem the ruthless onward rush of the Japanese. After the bombing of Rangoon by the Japanese in January, 1942, they advanced on Burma.

General Wavell was by now Commander-in-Chief, India, and General Harold Alexander was in command of the Burma Army. It was decided that he should withdraw the Army from Burma, across the border into India, and establish a defensive front there. Only there, in any case, could the force now be properly supported. Rangoon was abandoned in March and, before the monsoon began, the difficult withdrawal to India was started. They were pursued and harassed by a vicious enemy and it was to be costly in lives and materiel. The last elements of the Burma Army crossed into India early in May and established their defences. They had suffered considerably in a retreat through difficult terrain and in a frightful climate, with which at this stage the Japanese seemed to cope supremely well.

Stagnation largely followed the retreat, and fortunately, with the coming of the monsoon, major offensive activity ceased. The Japanese reinforced their army, and, although their lines of supply were very stretched, nevertheless proved how well they could manage with limited supplies. The British retrained, improved road and

rail communications, and carried out several operations which, though not all completely successful, established the pattern for both the tactics and logistics of the offensive that was to come. In particular, the future mode of transportation which was to outweigh all others in the operations came into being – supply by air. It was made possible once air superiority had been achieved by the tremendous efforts of the RAF. The initial RAF fighter squadrons, 135, 136, 261 and 607, who bore the brunt of the early Japanese attacks, were gradually reinforced with additional squadrons and re-equipped with improved aircraft. The RAF, with the Indian and American airforces to help, and their bomber force increasing, began to gain the upper hand from early in 1943.

Road communications, such as they were, ran largely from north to south, as did the mountain ranges, and these, with the Rivers Chindwin and Irrawaddy, were major obstacles to lateral movement. In the main, vehicles could not move off the roads and tracks, and in the monsoon from May to September movement by vehicle was restricted to the few all-weather roads. At that time land operations in the monsoon were considered virtually impossible, even by the Japanese. In the next two years, though, many of the problems brought about by these conditions were overcome.

On the central front the two main centres of British defence were based on Kohima and Imphal, which were linked by the Manipur road, leading back to the railway from Calcutta at Dimapur. This, the main supply link, was initially a single-track road 135 miles long, full of hair-raising uncertainties as it crossed a 5,000-foot mountain range. The railway also extended north from Dimapur to Ledo, and was the main supply line from India for General Stilwell's Chinese Army on the northern front. The railway also ran south to Chittagong and Cox's Bazar on the west

Members of the Black Watch march past their Hadrian glider on a North Burma landing strip, early 1944. (Royal Air Force Museum, Hendon)

coast, from where there was a road down to Akyab over the border into the Arakan, the southern front. The railway system, not designed for heavy usage, had become completely disorganized after the Japanese bombed Imphal. The differing gauges also meant that loads had to be transferred, and railway waggons had to be ferried across the Brahmaputra.

It was this geography and the paucity and condition of road and rail communications that was greatly to influence the tactics and maintenance of the recently formed British Fourteenth Army. Late in 1943, General Slim, from being a Corps Commander, took over command of Fourteenth Army, soon finding that the means of overcoming the problems of land communications was high on his list of requirements for defeating the Japanese. Because of the difficulty of road movement in the forward areas, where the Japanese also frequently established road blocks, units first learned to travel light, and, even more important, to move through the jungle. Pack mules were used extensively to provide transport within divisions.

In January, 1943, a drive was made down through the Arakan with the aim of capturing Akyab. This was a failure, as the force could not penetrate the Japanese defences and had to withdraw. In the north, another operation took place. This, with the support of General Wavell, was the

TOP LEFT *Gun crew of a 40mm AA gun watch their supplies being delivered to their Chindit column by a C47 Dakota aircraft, Burma, early 1944. (Leo Cooper Collection)*

BOTTOM LEFT *Chindits and their mules clearing air-dropped supplies, Burma, early 1944. (Leo Cooper Collection)*

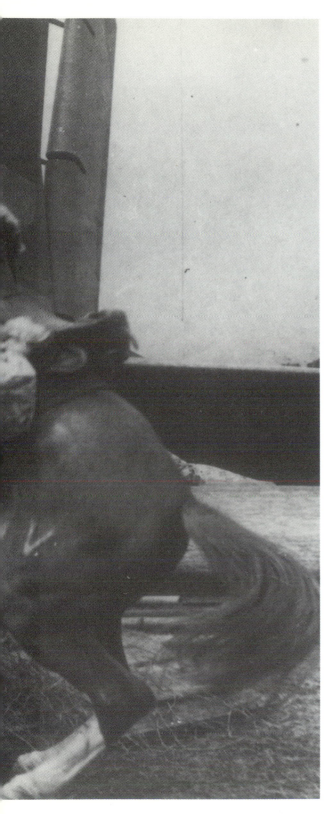

first venture by Major-General Orde Wingate's Chindits. In February, 1943, his force of 3,000 marched into the jungle towards the Shwebo area, transporting all their requirements on hundreds of pack mules, oxen and some elephants. Their task was to harass the enemy behind his lines and to cut the Mandalay–Myitkyina railway line, and possibly the Mandalay–Lashio line by crossing the Irrawaddy. It succeeded in cutting the Myitkyina railway line in numerous places, and inflicted many casualties on the enemy, but suffered considerable losses of its own in the process. Our special concern with this force is in the development of air supply. The force, throughout its time on this raid, from February to June, 1943, was entirely supplied by air drop, and this was almost 100% successful. Although critics of this operation have queried its overall material value, there is no doubt that it proved the feasibility of air supply and the inestimable value of this mode of transportation for the future, both in Burma and elsewhere. At this stage, though, a serious defect in the system was that the air transportation was one way only. There was no casualty evacuation by air in this operation; only those who could march out got out.

In August, 1943, South-East Asia Command was formed under Admiral Lord Louis Mountbatten, while General Sir Claude Auchinleck, as Commander-in-Chief, India, was responsible for the Indian Army, and directed and developed the great logistic base in India to support the campaign in Burma. The air and rail transportation systems were stepped up with the help of the Americans, and General Stilwell, now commanding a joint Chinese and American force in the north, was appointed Deputy Commander. Mountbatten's initial orders to his Staff contained the decree, 'We shall march, fight and fly through the monsoon'. This Fourteenth Army was to do.

In support of the American priority for keeping the Burma Road to China open, a second Wingate operation, in co-operation with General Stilwell's Chinese Force, was mounted at divisional strength on the northern front. Two brigades were flown in by gliders, towed by the

Loading a horse into a C47 Dakota aircraft, Burma, 1944. (Royal Air Force Museum)

The interior of the Dakota showing how the animals are restrained in flight using locally grown bamboo poles, Burma, 1944. (Royal Air Force Museum)

Men of The Argyll and Sutherland Highlanders leading a mule up the ramp into a United States Army Air Force DC3 Skytrain (US designation for Dakota), Burma, 1944. (Royal Air Force Museum)

American Air Force, while one marched in. The whole force, of British, Gurkhas and West Africans, in what was to be a most successful joint operation, was entirely maintained by the RAF and the American air forces. Regrettably, before the operation was completed, General Wingate was killed in an air crash.

The transport aircraft used in these operations was the C47 – the Dakota, which by the end of the War was as famous as its land counterpart – the Jeep. The essential overall air superiority which allowed uninterrupted air supply was maintained by the growing 3rd Tactical Air Force under the command of Air Marshal Sir John Baldwin, with British, American and Indian Air Force fighters and bombers.

An important additional transportation factor, though, was that additional means of casualty evacuation by air was achieved. This was largely due to the skill and effort of the American Army Air Force Colonel Philip Cochran, of No. 1 Air Commando, who provided the air transport support for Wingate. The system of transport aircraft snatching casevac gliders off the ground was perfected by his unit, and meant that casualties could be evacuated from many places where gliders had been used but planes themselves could not land. Light aircraft which could land on simple strips in jungle clearings were also brought into use.

In the Arakan a major operation was mounted by XVth Indian Corps commanded by Lieutenant-General Sir Philip Christison. Again the Force was greatly dependent on air supply, with transport on the ground being largely provided by pack mules. Although three of the Divisions involved – 5th, 7th Indian and 81st West African – were at one time cut off by the Japanese, they held out, with most of their maintenance being dropped by air. Some was also sent in by sea. Two relieving Divisions – the 26th and 36th – forced their way down the coast road and the first major defeat of the Japanese in Burma was achieved.

While the two British offensives outlined above were taking place, considerable work was going on to improve the land communications from India. Work on the Manipur road to make it two-way was undertaken with labour provided from the tea plantations in Assam, and road transport was then able to operate at a far greater

intensity to bring in supplies from the railhead at Dimapur. Hundreds of miles of road in the border areas were also improved by the Sappers. At the beginning of 1944 six United States Railway Battalions were brought in to militarize the 800 miles of the Bengal to Assam Railway, and in twelve months its capacity was more than doubled.

In March, 1944, the Japanese launched a major offensive against the central front. This was the most crucial battle of the campaign. With 100,000 troops, the Japanese advanced swiftly, cutting the Manipur road, and by April the bases of Kohima, with only some 3,500 defenders, and Imphal, whence 17th and 20th Indian Divisions had retired, were cut off. Over the next three months both bases were kept supplied by air and, in the case of Imphal, where transport aircraft could land, 5th Indian Division was flown in complete from the Arakan, to reinforce the area. During the course of the siege of Imphal, some 300 transport planes a day landed with stores and 30,000 wounded were evacuated.

At the same time as Imphal and Kohima were being supplied by air, a major reinforcement movement was taking place, and XXXIII Indian Corps was moved swiftly to Dimapur from southern India by air and rail to relieve Kohima. By May the Japanese had been defeated at Kohima and Imphal and the action started to clear them out of those parts of Manipur which they still occupied. By December General Slim was ready with the Fourteenth Army to cross the Chindwin and advance on Mandalay and south to Rangoon. For the offensive, the forward troops were to be supplied by air, but as XV Corps advanced down the Arakan, supply by sea also became possible. IV and XXXIII Corps were to advance down the central axis, with Stilwell's Chinese force in the north. Force 136, an allied clandestine organization concerned with infiltrating the Japanese puppet Burma National Army and winning them back to the Allies, also had patrols behind the Japanese lines. They were to gain the support of loyal Burmese, and eventually to ambush the retreating Japanese on both sides of the Sittang River. This force was also maintained by air drop and the use of light aircraft.

Although so much depended on supply by air

TOP LEFT *Convoy of Jeeps, Bedford and Chevrolet 15-cwt trucks in the Chin Hills, Burma, 1944. (IRCT)*

LOWER LEFT *An 0-6-0 locomotive being ferried across the Brahmaputra River in late 1944. Nine locomotives were sent to Myingyan, Burma, by way of the Manipur Road and Kalewa. (Museum of Army Transport)*

ABOVE *An 0-6-0 locomotive carried by Diamond T transporter on the Kalewa Road, Burma, 1944. (Museum of Army Transport)*

A Royal Air Force Lysander aircraft of 337 Squadron
on Bolo airstrip with supplies for Force 136, Burma,
1945. (Royal Air Force Museum)

L 5 aircraft being unloaded from an LCT near Akyab,
Burma, 1945. (Royal Air Force Museum)

Elephants moving supplies from Bolo airstrip. (Royal Air Force Museum)

for the offensive, a considerable land transport effort was now both possible and essential, as well as supply by sea. While most of the logistic MT on the L of C was provided by the RIASC, as were the mules, the RASC provided the specialist transport – tank transporters and DUKWs. Similarly, in the Indian Divisions, the RIASC provided all the logistic transport, as did the RASC for the British Divisions. The East African and West African Divisions also had their own respective ASC companies. There were three companies of RASC tank transporters, two of which supported the two Indian Tank Brigades, while one worked on the L of C. The movement of tanks on transporters was vital to preserve the track mileage until the River Irrawaddy was crossed. Ferrying the tanks forward was a hazardous and exhausting task for the companies concerned. DUKWs were used for all the river crossings and, in addition to their normal troop and cargo-carrying roles, also towed rafts built

from abandoned Japanese pontoons to ferry vehicles in the assault across the Irrawaddy.

As XV Corps advanced down through the Arakan, the Royal Navy, using assault craft, with warships in support, mounted an amphibious campaign down the coast, which was ultimately to end with the capture of Ramree Island by 26th Indian Division in January, 1945. Before this, the Navy had landed through the coastal chaungs (inlets), north of Ramree, some 18,000 troops, 14,500 tons of stores, 523 mules and 415 vehicles. The capture of Ramree Island enabled fighter airstrips to be built to support the amphibious

operation planned to capture Rangoon. In the event, on 2 May, 1945, as the monsoon rains descended, the amphibious force landed in Rangoon without opposition. The Japanese had fled, with the approach to their doorstep of IV and XXXIII Corps, who had fought every inch of the way down through Mandalay. The war in Burma was over.

It was a campaign in which transport by land, sea and air was controlled and utilized by determined commanders who were fully aware of both the problems and the means of solving them. Those responsible for operating the means played a vital part in the ultimate success achieved. Improvisation, co-operation and great flexibility were the hallmarks of success.

LEFT *Salvaged from the mudflats of the River Irrawaddy, the Irrawaddy Flotilla Company's SS* **Ontario** *was repaired and put into service on the supply line southwards from Mandalay, Burma, 1945. (Imperial War Museum)*

BELOW *Men of the Royal Norfolk Regiment arriving at the River Irrawaddy bridgehead by DUKW, 1945. (Leo Cooper Collection)*

North-west Europe

On 6 June, 1944, the Allies landed on the beaches of Normandy. Although the course of the War had taken the British Army worldwide, it was back in North-west Europe that it had to be won. The volume of transportation necessary in France and Germany was to surpass anything that had gone before, but the extent of the planning and preparations were to ensure that there was very little lacking to do the job. This is not to infer that nothing could go wrong, or that there was always sufficient transport. That is never so. However, the logistic transport arrangements were now based on the considerable experience gained in five years of war, and transportation from the very beginning matched the planned requirements. The vast manufacturing capacity of the United States had by now produced a great deal of the shipping, aircraft and vehicles needed for the task ahead. The training, too, within the UK fortress base, was intensive in all transportation spheres, and was designed to produce maximum effectiveness at the right time. Some two hundred RASC transport companies, equipped with every sort of vehicle from tank transporters to ambulances, were formed and allocated to formations, in addition to the companies of the divisional columns.

Most of the different types of logistic transport were from vehicle ranges that had already been tried and tested as the war progressed elsewhere, and the systems of control and operation of all elements of the transportation system were also fully proven and established. One exception to the types of transport that had proved so effective elsewhere, and that was now omitted from the order of battle, was animal transport. Mechanization for the Allies in North-west Europe was complete, but the horse was to return for further service after the War.

The greatest problem to be overcome was that of successfully landing and maintaining the force over the beaches of Normandy. The size and complexity of the sea transportation problem was enormous. Over 5,000 ships and craft were involved in the initial assault. It was the task of the Royal Navy to get the force there and to support the landings. More than 287,000 troops and 37,000 vehicles were pre-loaded into these mainly specialist craft for the assault landing. Water-proofing of these vehicles was in itself a consider-able task.

The RAF, in addition to providing the protec-tive air cover and assault attack for the force, were also involved in the transport role of conveying the 6th Airborne Division for their assault drops north-east of Caen, and subsequently of air supply to that Division and emergency drops to other formations. One hundred and eighty RASC air despatch crews were provided for the RAF squadrons involved in air supply, and they had a normal capability of despatching from the aircraft 360 tons a day.

Of the British Second Army, two British sea-borne divisions, the 50th and the 3rd, and one Canadian division, the 3rd, were the first to land, and these were built up to three British armoured divisions, (7th, 11th and Guards) and eight British infantry divisions, (3rd, 15th, 43rd, 49th, 50th, 51st, 53rd and 59th.) and the 6th Airborne, when the breakout from Normandy had been achieved by August. All landed with their integral logistic transport and by this time some 1,100,000 troops had been landed across the beaches.

The Transportation Service of the Royal Engineers was responsible for discharging and clearing over the beaches and through the ports all the incoming stores and vehicles, which amounted to some 900,000 tons and many

thousands of vehicles in the first few weeks of the landing. They were also responsible for the con-struction and repair of ports and railways, and for their operation. To provide the first port facilities, the British Mulberry harbour was constructed at Arromanches, (the Americans had a similar har-bour further west) and this started on 7 June, 1944. As the advance from Normandy took place in the next few months, civilian harbours were liberated, repaired and taken into use. However, until Mulberry was fully operative, discharge took place over the beaches, and Rhino Ferries and other craft of Inland Water Transport Units RE, and eleven DUKW Companies RASC, pro-

Men of 6th Airborne Division loading their bicycles into a Horsa glider, June, 1944. The Horsa could lift twenty-five men or three tons of equipment. (Airborne Forces Museum, Aldershot)

vided the means of accomplishing this. The quantities handled daily under difficult sea conditions, with frequent air attacks, can be judged by the fact that in 24 hours ending at 1800 on 11 June the RASC DUKWs carried 10,850 tons of stores from off-lying ships to the beaches, while in the first fourteen days the Rhino Ferries discharged 10,882 vehicles.

All the Engineer stores requirements for the whole operation into the heart of Germany had been preplanned, taking into account the assumed destruction of most bridges, docks and the railway system. RASC transport had to be provided for the carriage of this huge quantity of stores,

many being specialist vehicles such as bridging vehicles and tippers. On 19 June, 1944, there was a great storm off the Normandy coast, which blew for three days and nights. It destroyed the American prefabricated harbour to the west and damaged the British Mulberry and a lot of the craft used in discharging. Heroic rescue operations of stranded personnel took place in which craft of both the RE Inland Water Transport and

The Horsa glider used to convey the Commander of 6th
Airborne Division, Major-General 'Windy' Gale, to
Normandy during the night of 5/6 June, 1944. The two
parts of the fuselage could be separated by explosive charge
to allow swift extraction of vehicles and equipment.
(Airborne Forces Museum)

RIGHT Infantry wading ashore from their LSIs,
Normandy, 6 June, 1944. (Imperial War Museum)

BELOW Personnel, vehicles and equipment being ferried
ashore by Naval Landing (NL) pontoons, Normandy,
June, 1944. (Imperial War Museum)

RASC DUKWs ferrying stores from shipping laying off the Normandy beach, June, 1944. (IRCT)

General B. L. Montgomery, Commander-in-Chief 21 Army Group, visiting Beach Group staff at Port-en-Bessin, Normandy, soon after the landings, June, 1944. (Imperial War Museum)

the RASC Motor Boat Companies took part. The immediate task of restoration of the vital facilities fell to the Royal Engineers. By 23 June stores were being discharged from ships over the first pier, and casualties could be loaded directly on to hospital ships alongside. The American Mulberry was not repaired, but parts were used to improve the British Mulberry.

An innovative transportation system for petrol was a 'pipeline under the ocean' *PLUTO*, laid from England to Normandy. The small town of Port-en-Bessin was captured by D+1 and became the initial bulk petrol port. Storage tanks were erected at the terminal and the petrol was either packed into jerricans, now the standard petrol container, and carried forward in normal load carriers, or in bulk tankers until the overland pipelines were constructed.

By the beginning of September the British Second Army was advancing north-east. The First Canadian Army's task was to capture the heavily defended Channel ports, and they were taken into use as they were freed. By early in September it was possible to close down unloading operations across the beaches. The logistic support of the Armies was by road and rail, rail being taken into use as it was repaired, and engines and rolling stock brought in to replace those which had been destroyed. By the end of August a rail L of C was working from Bayeux to railheads as far forward as Rouen, and was extended as the advance continued.

Austin K 2 ambulances evacuating casualties to a hospital ship alongside Mulberry Harbour, Normandy. (Museum of Army Transport)

Pipeline being laid alongside the road towards the forward area, June, 1944. Chevrolet tipping truck and Fordson 15-cwt trucks using the road. (Imperial War Museum)

When Second Army had reached the line of the Meuse–Escaut Canal, it was agreed that the Rhine bridge at Arnhem should be assaulted and temporarily held by airborne forces until a ground link-up could be effected and the advance continued through Holland. The plan was known as Operation Market Garden. The major airborne assault on Arnhem by the 1st Airborne Division, commanded by Major-General Roy Urquhart, took place over the three days of 17–19 September. Ideally it should have taken place in a single day, but there were insufficient aircraft for one lift. This undoubtedly contributed to the subsequent failure of the operation.

The transport aircraft to carry the Paratroops were provided by ten squadrons of 38 Group RAF, and those to tow the glider force by six squadrons of 46 Group. During the period that 1st Airborne Division held the bridge, it was main-tained by air supply drops, under fierce AA fire. On 19 September a Dakota of 271 Squadron RAF piloted by Flight-Lieutenant David Lord, DFC, RAF, who had previously served in Burma, flying Dakotas in support of Wingate's Chindits, was involved in an action over Arnhem for which he was to be awarded a posthumous Victoria Cross. His plane, whose crew included four RASC despatchers, was hit by heavy AA fire over Arnhem, but he completed his air supply task in his blazing plane and stayed with it to try and save the crew. Only one member of the crew, who was able to use his parachute, survived. The rest were killed when the plane crashed.

Bedford 3-ton, 600-gallon petrol tankers drawing bulk
fuel from a petrol point, Normandy, June, 1944.
(IRCT)

Men of The Wiltshire Regiment crossing the River Seine
in an assault boat, August, 1944. (Leo Cooper Collection)

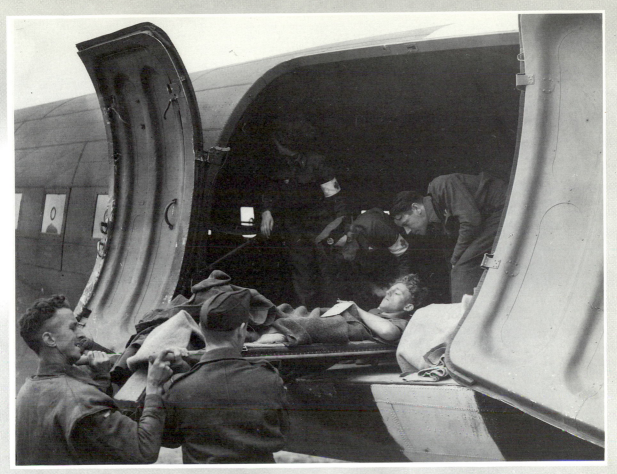

Casualty being loaded into a Dakota aircraft operating
from a Normandy airstrip. Arriving back in a UK hospital
in so short a time considerably increased the chances of
recovery from wounds. (Imperial War Museum)

BELOW Royal Air Force Stirling tugs and Hamilcar
gliders lined up at a United Kingdom airfield ready for
take-off for the airborne assault on Arnhem, Holland
(Operation Market Garden), 17 September, 1944.
Hamilcar gliders could lift forty men or seven tons of
equipment. (Airborne Forces Museum)

Flight-Lieutenant Lord, RAF, and RASC air despatch
crew in the fuselage of a C 47 aircraft. He was awarded
a posthumous Victoria Cross during the Arnhem
operation for his action in pressing on with his supply
drop although his aircraft was mortally damaged by AA
fire. Two of his crew and four RASC air despatchers
also perished. Flying Officer Harry King was blown
from the aircraft, managed to open his parachute and
survived. This photograph was taken on a resupply
mission in Burma where he was awarded the
Distinguished Flying Cross. (IRCT)

The gallant survivors of Arnhem, totally out-numbered and outgunned by the German armoured forces, had to be withdrawn on 26 September. By December, despite this setback, Second Army was lined up along the Meuse. Plans for the battle of the Rhineland were in an advanced state of preparation when the Germans launched a surprise counter-offensive on 13 December against the Americans in the Ardennes. The ensuing battle was hard-fought, against fanatical German opposition and in frightful weather conditions, but the British and American pincer movement was eventually successful. By the beginning of March 21 Army Group was established along the western bank of the Rhine. On 23 March the crossing of the Rhine was made and the end was in sight.

The logistic effort to maintain Second Army in its advance from Normandy to the Rhine had been enormous. Although there had appeared to be sufficient transport to carry out the predicted tasks, in the event, as always, it was only the indefatigable efforts of all those in the transportation agencies that enabled the tremendous momentum of the Army to be sustained. Every sort of transport on land, water and in the air had been used to its limits. Every sort of load had been carried, and delivered to wherever required. Unlike many earlier campaigns, the carefully planned and organized transportation effort had met the requirement.

1st Airborne Division landing at Wolfeze, near Arnhem, 17 September, 1944. (Imperial War Museum)

*M 29c Weasels disembarking from an LCT of
Force T, Royal Navy, at Walcheren, Netherlands,
1 November, 1944, during operations to clear the River
Scheldt and open up the port of Antwerp, Belgium. The
Weasel, a tracked amphibian weighing only 2.71 tons,
could carry half a ton in rivers and estuaries. (Royal Naval
Museum)*

*Members of The Highland Light Infantry and The
Argyll and Sutherland Highlanders crossing a Class 40
(bears loads up to 40 tons) bridge over the River Raisal
at Maergestel, Netherlands, 28 October, 1944. The vehicle
on the bridge is a White (US) scout car often used as
ambulances particularly in armoured formations. A
Bren carrier in the foreground. (Leo Cooper Collection)*

The 3-ton Bedford QL truck with troop-carrying body
(TCV). These vehicles appeared in most theatres and
were capable of carrying a platoon of infantry, 36 men,
almost anywhere that a tank could go. (IRCT)

TOP LEFT *Landing Vehicles Tracked (LVTs),*
Buffaloes, with men of The Cheshire Regiment landing
on the east bank of the River Rhine, 24 March, 1944.
The demolished bridge is the Wesel railway bridge. The
LVT 4 weighed 16.5 tons and could carry four tons.
(Imperial War Museum)

BOTTOM LEFT *The 1000th British-built locomotive to*
be sent to Europe since D Day on 6 June, 1944. This
2-10-0 freight locomotive is now in the museum at
Utrecht, Netherlands. (Museum of Army Transport)

7

Transport in the Years of
Major Peace and Minor Wars

THE PERIOD of some forty years covered by this chapter has not conformed to the same extreme pattern of retrenchment which followed the First World War, though many involved in military refurbishment programmes might wish to deny this. There have, however, been many threatening political situations throughout the world, which have caused the Government to initiate Army intervention. The resulting campaigns, or confrontations, broadly supported by the British public, have themselves enabled some major developments to take place, in order that the Army could properly fulfil its role. Furthermore, the Army's overall activities have not only produced a development need for its own logistic transport, but also in the other two Services for the sort of transport to be used by them for carrying the Army.

The Army has served in some forty countries and there have been sixteen campaigns for which campaign medals have been awarded since the Second World War. It is not surprising, therefore, that a wealth of experience has continued to be available to those concerned with the development, organization and control of transport. In addition to actual campaigns, other overall factors, such as the NATO defence policy, advancement and cost of modern technology, streamlining of logistic systems and commercial developments, have all affected the types and role of transport in the Army.

The British Army of the Rhine (BAOR), with Northern Army Group, provides the main

British Army link with NATO. It has been in existence under gradually changing conditions since 1945. In its deterrent role, BAOR remains the largest continuous committment for the Army, and much of the training and equipment trials of the Army, including transport, takes place in West Germany. Also, because of the size of BAOR and the fact that it is a family station, its overall logistic support is of considerable magnitude and variety. The provision, operation and control of transport plays a not inconsiderable part within this task, and much that goes on in BAOR is reflected in Army transport activities everywhere. A brief examination of these activities helps to provide overall examples of the modes and their development trends and usage. Some of the campaigns are brought in to indicate use of particular transport under operational conditions or in situations special to the campaign.

When the Second World War ended, the British Army in Europe was spread through West Germany, Austria, Northern Italy and Trieste. Movement of troops back to UK both for demobilization and leave was by rail and cross-channel ferry from the Hook of Holland. With the large numbers involved, this was a major operation. All the trains and ships were civilian-manned and controlled on the ground by Movement Control personnel of the Royal Engineers. Special trains on scheduled services covered all the major British garrisons in Germany and were designated by colours according to destinations – red, blue and white. The Medloc train was started

to take home troops from north Italy immediately after the war, and initially went through Switzerland, which required special dispensation arranged by the Movements staff, until the tunnels from Italy to Austria could be repaired. The train that is still running today is the British Military Train – the Berliner. It ran daily until 1960 from the Hook of Holland, with a break during the Berlin blockade in 1948–49, and now runs daily through the Russian Zone, between Hanover and Berlin. As soon as families were allowed to join their husbands in North-West Europe, including Berlin, they travelled by the same means.

In June, 1948, the Russians blockaded the overland routes into West Berlin. Plans had been made for the RAF to supply the garrison in the British Zone of Berlin by air in the event of this happening, but the extent and length of the blockade had not been anticipated. In a short time it became a joint operation with the Americans, who provided the larger part of the lift; not only were the

The 'Berliner', the British Military Train that has run daily, except Christmas Day and during the blockade of 1948/1949, to and from Berlin through the corridor in the German Democratic Republic. Seen here at Charlottenburg Station, West Berlin, with part of the military staff which includes an Officer Commanding, a Train Conducting Warrant Officer, Russian interpreter, a Postal and Courier NCO and a military guard. (62 Squadron, Royal Corps of Transport)

other allied garrisons supplied, but the whole of the civilian population as well. In the British Zone of West Germany the operation required a large ground organization for transport and load control, and this was provided by the RASC elements of the Army Air Transport Organization in support of the RAF's air transport effort.

Work on the development of a new range of vehicles was started soon after the war, and the philosophy of a common range of military engines that could be adapted for a variety of vehicles was introduced. The engines were Rolls

20 Company RASC on Horse Guards Parade, London, c1955. The task of this unit at the time was to provide transport support for the Ministry of Defence, the War Office, and Headquarters, London District and London Units. It also provided Her Majesty The Queen's Baggage Train. In 1965 it became 20 Squadron Royal Corps of Transport and now, in addition, supports the Navy and Air Departments. Vehicles in this photograph range from a Rolls Royce Phantom, Austin Princess, Humber Super Snipe, Standard Vanguard, Austin Hereford, Ford Popular to the Landrover. The unit is now equipped with a more limited range of modern vehicles; an example appears on page 204. (Not covered in text) (IRCT)

An RAF York aircraft preparing for take-off at Wunsdorf, Germany, during the Berlin Airlift, Operation Plainfare, 26 June, 1948–30 September, 1949. Besides maintaining the Allied Forces in Berlin which was the original intention, the population of West Berlin was also supplied. A total of 2,050,608 tons was lifted by 296,030 sorties by Allied aircraft. (Royal Air Force Museum)

Royce, and were known as the 'B' Range, with three sizes of engines, B40, B60 and B80, and vehicle trials started in the early 1950s. Unfortunately, although the vehicles had some good design features, the desire to make them 'all singing and all dancing' meant that they were too complicated and proved to be unreliable. The vehicle designed to replace the Jeep, which was now too expensive to buy from the United States, was the Champ, with the B40 engine. Hardly less expensive, but no dollars were involved. Nothing could make it as popular as the Jeep, and it was a far from successful vehicle, but it remained in service until the mid-60s. The other vehicles in the range were considered unsuccessful early on, and were discontinued. The ultimate replacement of the Champ by the Land Rover was considered a great advance by the average user, but was not accepted

into general service by the Army until 1956, and has continued successfully in various forms ever since.

In 1953 trials took place in BAOR with vehicles to replace the old 3-ton Bedford OY and QLs which had given such excellent service in the War. The Bedford RL became its successor and the standard logistic load carrier. Other makes, such as the Commer, were used as tippers. In 1968 the RL was upgraded to 4-ton capacity, but the term '3-tonner' among drivers took a long time to die. Its successor, taken into service in 1971, was the

The Austin Champ in difficulties again! This 'all singing, all dancing' vehicle had a short Service life, much to the relief of all those people who had to operate it. This photograph was taken in BAOR c1952. (Lieutenant-Colonel M. H. G. Young, late RCT)

The current field-force ambulance, the Landrover 4 × 4. (School of Transportation)

Bedford MK, with a number of refinements, but it had taken eleven years to materialize.

In 1969, because of the cost of producing special military vehicles, the Army Department produced a new doctrine for logistic load carriers, based on their cross-country capability. There were three categories – high, medium and low mobility. In general terms, the category, and the type of vehicle within it, depended upon the logistic environment in which the vehicle would be expected to operate. An example of a high-mobility vehicle, introduced in 1961, and still in service, is the Alvis Stalwart. It was issued to replace some of the 3-ton vehicles, both in combat arms, and in divisional units of the RASC. It is probably still the best cross-country 5-ton load-carrier of its class in the world. Because of expense, though, nobody will ever have enough of

this type of vehicle, and, like many specialized vehicles, its employment requires careful allocation and control.

It was in the Korean War, 1950–1953, that the British Army, using very much the same well-tried vehicles and systems as in the Second World War, was introduced to the logistic helicopter by the Americans. It was an introduction that was to endure and flourish, albeit slowly. In September, 1951, two British battalions were cut off for 48 hrs by a flood, and the Divisional RASC were able to have some 6,500 pounds of rations and ammunition flown in to them by United States' helicopters. This was their only logistic operational use by the British Army, but it was a start. An

An Alvis Stalwart in the Western Aden Protectorate c1958. Beside its rough terrain capabilities, this amphibious vehicle can carry four tons in river and estuary waters. (IRCT)

Centurion tank of 8th King's Royal Irish Hussars climbs the bank of the Imjin River carrying men of the Royal Northumberland Fusiliers. Korean Campaign, June, 1950–July, 1953. (Leo Cooper Collection)

exercise using twelve Sikorsky H-MC helicopters, loaned by the Americans for the task when hostilities ended, together with a study of their operational use by the Americans throughout the campaign, convinced the British that helicopters had a future! In April, 1955, the Joint Experimental Helicopter Unit (JEHU) was formed in the UK. It was a joint Army/RAF unit and was involved in operations in the Suez campaign and against EOKA in Cyprus with Sycamore Mark 14 and Whirlwind Mark 2 helicopters.

The unit also took part in exercises in BAOR. In mid-1959 came the surprise decision to disband the unit, and, in what was to be a milestone in the use of helicopters in logistic support of the Army, the task was handed over to the RAF. Some fixed-wing light logistic aircraft were to remain with the Army Air Corps, in flights largely piloted by the RASC, (later Royal Corps of Transport) until 1974.

INSET *A United States of America Army helicopter delivering ammunition to a Royal Artillery gun position in Korea, 1952. (Imperial War Museum)*

A Whirlwind helicopter of the Joint Experimental Helicopter Unit, c1958, lifting palleted stores during an exercise in the United Kingdom. This aircraft could lift one-ton packs. Only four of these aircraft bore Army markings, the others were operated by the Royal Navy and Royal Air Force. (School of Transportation, RCT – Crown Copyright))

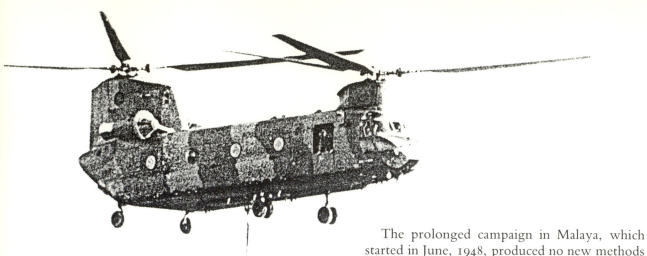

An RAF Chinook helicopter lifting a fully laden 4-ton truck c1987. The all-up weight of this load is nine tons. (IRCT)

The prolonged campaign in Malaya, which started in June, 1948, produced no new methods of land transport, but the air supply lessons learned in Burma were quickly adapted for Malaya and air supply became the main means of logistic support for the troops operating in the jungle. The Royal Air Force, Royal Australian Air Force and Royal New Zealand Air Force all provided aircraft and crews during the campaign, and the despatchers were provided from Air Despatch Units of the RASC. A variety of transport aircraft was used during the campaign, and very large quantities of stores were dropped, as many as seventy-five dropping zones operating at one time. Initially the well-proven Dakota was used, and for the RAF this was replaced by the very suitable Valetta in 1952. In 1955 the RNZAF flew the successful Bristol Freighters, but the RAF's trials with the Hastings were not successful, as the aircraft were insufficiently manoeuvrable for jungle dropping. For a period a squadron of RN helicopters also assisted with this air support.

The Malayan Emergency continued until 1960, and, although there was no significant change in land vehicles, a new permanent element of drivers for logistic vehicles was formed in Malaya and Singapore at this time. This was the Gurkha Army Service Corps, formed in July, 1958, which was to become a permanent part of the British Army in the Brigade of Gurkhas. During this whole period, too, many of the RASC MT Companies had Malay as well as British drivers, some having served before the Second World War, and these were enlisted into the British Army and integrated into the units. A number reached commissioned rank. Ultimately many formed the basis of the Malay Service Corps, when Malaya became independent.

*Saracen APCs manned by the Gurkha Transport
Regiment, Hong Kong, 1980s. (Photograph by Captain
P. J. Brown, RCT)*

Emplaning in a RAF VC 10 for an overseas garrison from RAF Brize Norton c1976. (IRCT)

Between the late 1950s and early 1960s major transportation changes affecting BAOR and all overseas stations took place. These were basically the change from sea to air movement for all routine transportation of troops and their families. BAOR was the first to be affected. The use of the civil shipping route between Harwich and the Hook of Holland, and, in BAOR, the land movement to and from the port by military train service was discontinued, being replaced by Air Trooping. In the UK normal civil airports were used for the new service, Gatwick initially, and then Luton, and in Germany a mixture of civil and RAF airfields. A more poignant change, however, was that of the abolition of the troopship for routine movement and its replacement by long-distance air trooping. Both RAF and civil contract aircraft were used. With the arrival at Southampton on 18 November, 1962 of the troopship *Oxfordshire* from the Far East there ended three hundred years of sea trooping. But sea trooping was, in fact, far from finished, and,

although the troopship as so many soldiers over generations had known it had departed, more sophisticated shipping was to become available for operational movement. On one occasion, also, bigger and more luxurious troopships were to make a temporary appearance in a time of need. The more sophisticated vessels for transporting the Army were the Landing Ships Logistic (LSL), and by 1967 six were in service, taking their names from King Arthur's Knights. These remarkable vessels of some 5,000 tons gross can carry a squadron of tanks or equivalent number of vehicles, and for short voyages, a battalion of infantry with all their equipment. Up until March, 1970, these vessels were operated and crewed by the British India Steam Navigation Company, on the Army's behalf, through the Board of Trade, Sea Transport Branch. They were then taken over by the Royal Navy as Royal

Fleet Auxiliary ships, but remained tasked by the Army. Other new Army vessels were to follow, though somewhat smaller. They were, however, to be Army-manned by crews from the RCT. These vessels were the Landing Craft Logistic, with a length of 240 feet and beam of 42 feet. They replaced the Landing Craft Tank, which had provided such good service during the War but were then over thirty years old.

In 1965 a major change took place in the organization and operation of logistic transport in the Army, as a result of the recommendations of the War Office McLeod Committee. The Royal Corps of Transport (RCT) was formed. The new Corps was established from the transport element of the RASC and the transportation elements (Ports, Inland Water Transport and Railways, other than civil engineering and mechanical repairs) of the Royal Engineers. It was to be responsible for the operation and control of all logistic transport and movement. All the other functions of the RASC, including Supplies and Petroleum, passed to the RAOC. The other Corps concerned with all mechanical repair, REME, remained unchanged. This conformed with the Army Council's (now Army Board)

policy of one Corps in the Army for supplying, one for moving and one for repairing. Whilst initially the new organizations involved considerable readjustment, the changes were quickly digested, though not perhaps without a few historical qualms.

The confrontation with Indonesia in Brunei and North Borneo, which started in 1962, provides an opportunity to introduce a new form of transportation, the hovercraft. At this time a tri-Service Unit to carry out an evaluation of the hovercraft produced by the British Hovercraft Corporation was established at Lee-on-Solent. By early 1965 a Joint Service Hovercraft Unit – Far East was evaluating two SRN5 hovercraft in Borneo. These carried out extensive and varied trials under full operational conditions, with a crew of RASC officers and soldiers. The craft were used for a variety of logistic tasks and were integrated into the supply organization for a period. They also moved patrols up the rivers and carried out exercises with the Royal Marines.

Emplaning in an RAF Tristar of 216 Squadron RAF for an exercise in Canada, Brize Norton, 1987. (Royal Air Force Brize Norton).

ABOVE *The SS* **Empire Fowey** *passing Kabrit Point at the southern end of the Great Bitter Lake in the Suez Canal, c1954. This troopship was formerly the North German Lloyds Far East Express Line* **Potsdam**. *The ship was affiliated to the Royal Engineers. (Painting by Colonel R. C. Gabriel, late Royal Engineers)*

TOP RIGHT *The Landing Ship Logistic (LSL)* **Sir Galahad** *operated by the Royal Fleet Auxiliary on behalf of the Army Department unloading into the Freight Section of the Joint Movements Centre, Hong Kong, c1970. This ship was later lost during the Falklands Campaign. (IRCT – Crown Copyright)*

RIGHT *A Landing Craft Logistic (LCL). An ocean-going vessel with a range of 4000 miles and has a complement of four RCT officers, eight warrant officers and senior non-commissioned officers and twenty-four soldiers. It can lift five main battle tanks or eleven 8-ton cargo vehicles or thirty-six 20 ft ISO containers. (Ministry of Defence – Crown Copyright)*

Elsewhere the craft had successful trials under desert and arctic conditions, and in Australia and much of the Far East. In 1974, despite the un-doubted, proven capability of these craft, their use was abandoned on grounds of economy.

Water transport was very much in use in Brunei and Borneo, and both LSLs and the RASC-crewed smaller Landing Craft Tank

TOP LEFT *A Ramped Craft Logistic (RCL). A small landing craft for use in coastal waters and ports. It is commanded by an RCT staff sergeant with a crew of six soldiers and can lift 100 soldiers or four 8-ton cargo vehicles or four 20 ft ISO containers. (Ministry of Defence – Crown Copyright)*

LEFT *SRN 6 Hovercraft unloading stores at a platoon base at Sungei Serudong, close to the Indonesian Border, Borneo, 1965. (Colonel R. N. Harris, late RCT)*

ABOVE *SRN 6 Hovercraft on a NATO exercise in the Arctic lifting a Sno-Cat tracked carrier, 1966. (Colonel R. N. Harris, late RCT)*

(LCT) operated there. At this time Royal Engineer Inland Water Transport units had Ramped Powered Lighters (RPL) and smaller craft working from the port. Infantry patrols were also carried up the rivers in small craft. The RE and RASC Water Transport elements were to come together in July, 1965, as part of the Royal Corps of Transport, while the campaign was still active.

Once again air supply was to be the mainstay of the logistic support for the troops in the jungles of Borneo. The RAF, now flying Beverley transport planes as well as the older Valettas, operated from two airfields at Labuan and Kuching. 3 Army Air Supply Organization (later 15 Air Despatch Regiment RCT) provided all the air despatchers, assisted by Air Maintenance Platoons of the RAOC. Some eighteen infantry battalions were supported in the jungle, and between January, 1965, and October, 1966, almost twenty-two thousand tons of stores were dropped. The RAF also operated short-range transport aircraft – both single and twin Pioneers – and now had a fully established logistic helicopter force of Belvedere, Wessex and Whirlwind helicopters. In addition, the Royal Navy had Wessex helicopters, and the Army Air Corps Sioux helicopters, as well as their RASC/RCT fixed-wing flight of Beaver aircraft.

Although in Borneo there were no special land transport vehicles in use, and, because of the lack of roads, air and water transport predominated, there was still a considerable task for road transport. It is a matter of interest that much of the logistic transport in Borneo was driven by Gurkhas of the Gurkha Army Service Corps, only recently formed and now proving their worth on operations. The Gurkhas provided a continuous element, from their base in Singapore and Malaya, other British elements of the RASC being sent out from the UK on rotation.

From the late Sixties onwards there was continuous progress in the RCT in developing both new types of vehicles and in transportation systems to conform to those that were now appearing in the civil transport world. Plans for the re-development of Marchwood Military Port

in Southampton Water as part of the Army's transportation, were laid down, and although they were to take some twenty years to come to fruition, the port was to see continuous increase in usage and in importance over the years. Some considerable improvements have already been made to the facilities, and major work is continuing to make it a fine example of a multi-purpose port. In particular, containerization for the movement of stores between RAOC depots in the UK and BAOR was started, using Marchwood, and gradually the system was developed to its full potential. Container-handling facilities and long-term contract hire of vehicles to carry containers within the UK followed. The berthing facilities were improved for the LSLs, and a Roll On, Roll Off facility constructed for vehicles. All movement of tanks and vehicles for BAOR now takes place through Marchwood, using the LSLs or the two RCT LCLs.

Patrol of the Royal Ulster Rifles (RUR) on the River Katibas, Sarawak, May, 1964, during the Borneo Campaign. (Royal Ulster Rifles Regimental Museum)

ABOVE *Her Majesty's Army Vessel* **Arromanches**, *an LCT of 46 Squadron RCT, based at Singapore, with supplies for the British Force, Brunei, 1966. (IRCT)*

RIGHT *A Beaver aircraft of 130 Flight RCT over Singapore, 1965. (IRCT)*

BELOW *A container trailer reversing into an LSL at Marchwood Military Port, c1987. (Ministry of Defence – Crown Copyright)*

In BAOR matching systems for the movement of containers sent from Marchwood through Antwerp were evolved, and door-to-door service for the movement of unit and family equipment and kit are now standard practice. There are two very effective civilian organizations in BAOR which have an important role within the RCT for operating transport in Germany. These are the German-manned Mobile Civilian Transport Groups (MCTG) and the Mixed Service Organization (MSO), who are found from ethnic minorities who stayed on in Germany after the War, especially Poles and those from the Baltic countries. The MCTG provides the transport units which carry out much of the routine local transport duties in BAOR, including driving the buses for the British school children. The MSO have a more operational role, and, in particular, drive a proportion of the tank transporters for the armoured regiments.

The continuous development of a wide range of vehicles has seen the gradual re-equipping of the Field Force units in BAOR from the mid-seventies. Specialist training for much of the new range of vehicles is carried out on an 'All Arms' basis at the Army School of Mechanical Transport at Leconfield, near Beverley in East Yorkshire. It has a mixed training fleet of some seven hundred vehicles, and in addition to comprehensive vehicle management and driver training, maintains a worldwide liaison with foreign armies and civilian organizations on driver training techniques and vehicle administration. Some of the new range of logistic vehicles includes the replacement for the Thornycroft 'Mighty Antar' tank transporter, which has served the Army so well. Its successor is the Scammel Commander, a considerably more powerful vehicle, to carry the Challenger tank. The Bedford 8-tonne vehicle

A Bedford school bus with a Mixed Service Organization (MSO) driver delivering children to a British Forces Education Service (BFES) school, BAOR, c1982. (IRCT)

Part of the fleet of training vehicles at the Army School of Mechanical Transport (ASMT) Leconfield, Yorkshire, c1986. (IRCT)

with a turbo-charged engine and the 10-tonne Leyland Crusader already provide heavier lift with greater mobility and many of the vehicles are fitted with cranes to lift palletized loads on and off vehicles. More sophisticated vehicles with built-in equipment for handling whole loads of pallets at once are now beginning to appear. Many other types of specialist vehicles have also been replaced and the logistic fleet of vehicles is now very different to that at the end of the Second World War. It can undoubtedly be said that the organization behind the transport is highly trained and well organized to manage it.

TOP LEFT *The Thornycroft Antar, the replacement for the Diamond 'T' as the tank transporter of the British Army. This photograph, taken in 1954, shows the vehicle operated by the Military Civilian Transport Group (MCTG) carrying a Conqueror tank. (Ministry of Defence – Crown Copyright)*

BOTTOM LEFT *The successor to the Antar. The Scammell Commander 6 × 4 wheeled tractor and semi-trailer, 98-ton gross combination weight. (School of Transportation, RCT – Crown Copyright)*

ABOVE *A Bedford TM 8-tonne truck with Atlas built-in crane. (School of Transportation, RCT – Crown Copyright)*

LEFT *A Bedford 14-tonne truck loaded with ISO container. (School of Transportation, RCT – Crown Copyright)*

Demountable Rack Off-Loading and Pick-Up System (DROPS). This system is being taken into service in 1989/1990. The flat rack can carry fifteen tons of NATO pallets or unit loads and has been developed to increase the total vehicle lift capacity for ammunition and explosives. It is anticipated that various load modules will be introduced later. (School of Transportation, RCT – Crown Copyright)

At the end of the Second World War there were 17,000 women of the ATS serving in the RASC, most of whom were drivers. In February, 1949, as the ATS were running down and were being demobilized, the Women's Royal Army Corps came into being and women drivers started to form a permanent part of RASC MT units of the Regular Army. Although training separately to start with, there was a gradual integration and by the time that the RCT was formed in 1965, WRAC drivers were to be found in many units in BAOR and UK, driving all but the heaviest range of vehicles. Although WRAC clerks served in the RASC, these were mainly in the Supply Branch, with some MT clerks, but in the Seventies, as a result of an Army Board decision, WRAC were accepted into RCT units as Movement Controllers, both in the Regular Army and the TA. WRAC officers are now also filling RCT officers' appointments in a variety of RCT units and attend many of the RCT technical courses. Today the WRAC are as much at home driving and controlling many of the Army's vehicles, in all but Field Force units, as their RCT male counterparts, and play an essential role in the Movements organization.

In November, 1956, the politically calamitous operations against Egypt, resulting from the failure of British and French diplomatic efforts to have the Suez Canal 'reinternationalized', was nevertheless a combined operation of some significance. The amphibious and airborne operations were well carried out, and, irrespective of the ultimate result, the combined force landing was completely successful. Within the overall plan, the transportation aspects generally worked well. While no new types of transport were involved, it was the first time that a considerable force of helicopters had been used by the British Army for ship-to-shore movement, for both men and materiel. It also showed the effectiveness of

A Daimler limousine staff car of 20 Squadron RCT. The driver is Corporal Chris Coon, WRAC. These vehicles are employed carrying senior military officers of the British Forces, visitors from foreign Forces and members of the Royal Family when visiting British military units. (Major N. J. Sutton, The Gordon Highlanders)

*Lieutenant N. Notley, WRAC, TA, supervising the
detraining of the Household Cavalry at Bangor,
Gwynedd, Wales to take part in the Investiture of HRH
The Prince of Wales, June, 1969. British Rail ceased
to provide horse boxes after this event so that moves of
horsed units now take place by road. (Major N. A. Notley,
WRAC, TA)*

casualty evacuation by helicopter direct from the
assault area back to ship.

In the Sixties there was considerable military
activity in the Gulf, including operations in the
Radfan and the British withdrawal from Aden in
1967. This withdrawal, carried out under difficult
conditions of civil strife and armed revolt in
Aden, was followed by a build-up in Bahrain and
Sharjah, and operations in support of the Gulf
States. In all these operations, which included the
use of some hired animal transport, there was an
opportunity to try out some existing types of
transport under totally different conditions. In
Aden the Alvis Stalwart high-mobility load
carrier, which was still under trials, was heavily
involved in operations in the Radfan and proved
its capability in the desert scrub and high tempera-
ture conditions. At the same time the Belvedere
logistic helicopters operated by the RAF, for
landed delivery, and the fixed-wing aircraft,
Beverleys, Argosys, Twin Pioneer, and Beavers
for dropping, were fully employed in the Radfan,
and later in the Gulf. They were supported by an
RASC Air Despatch Company (later Air Despatch Squadron RCT). Finally, the withdrawal
from Aden included the use of four of the six LSLs
then in service, still operated by British India
Steam Navigation Company, four of the now
elderly LSTs, also civilian-crewed, and one RCT
LCT. There was a Royal Naval Task Force in
support, and all the operations through the docks
were handled by the Joint Services Port Unit,
with additional elements of a Port Regiment and
Port Squadron RCT. Some 57,000 tons of stores
and over 2,000 vehicles were evacuated, and the
Army's long, perhaps reluctant, association with
Aden was over.

The operations against the Mau Mau in Kenya
between October, 1952, and the end of 1956
produce two new examples of types of transport

TOP RIGHT *A Centurion tank of 6th Royal Tank
Regiment (RTR) leaving the doors of a LST at Port
Said, Egypt, during Operation Musketeer, December,
1956. (Imperial War Museum)*

RIGHT *A casualty of the battle of Port Said arriving by
helicopter on the flight-deck of HMS* **Sea Eagle**,
December, 1956. (Imperial War Museum)

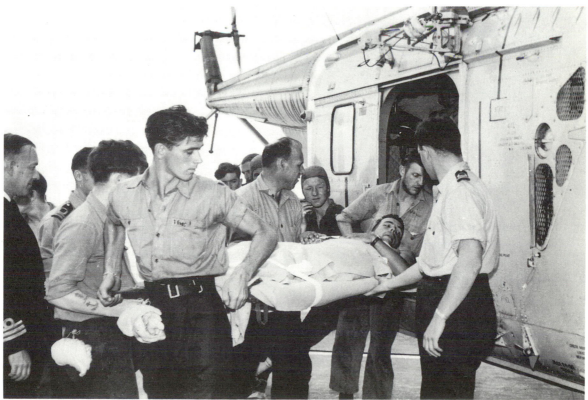

Captain John Fleming, Royal Artillery, with his Sioux
helicopter on the summit of a jebel in the Radfan,
Arabian Gulf, 1964. He was killed shortly after this
photograph was taken when his aircraft was hit by gunfire.
(Leo Cooper Collection)

An RAF Beverley aircraft landing at Thumeir airstrip,
Southern Arabia, 1965. (Royal Air Force Museum)

An RAF Wessex helicopter lifting a 105mm howitzer into position, Western Aden Protectorate, 1965. (Royal Air Force Museum)

OVERLEAF *An RAF Beverley aircraft being unloaded by RASC personnel at Thumeir airstrip, March 1965. (Royal Air Force Museum)*

operating under different conditions. Much of the logistic road transport in Kenya during this emergency was provided by the East African Army Service Corps (EAASC), but they also at this time still had animal transport. An EAASC Mule Company supported the force deployed in the Aberdare Range and Mount Kenya areas. The operations took place at altitudes of between 10,000 and 12,000 feet, where only mules could operate to provide land transport and again proved their versatility, this time with East African muleteers. It was not certain how the mules would react to working at these heights, but with a reduced load of one hundred pounds, and a tot of rum in their grain, they soon got used to the exceptional conditions. A different form of air supply was also utilized to make drops into small forest clearings. Light planes – Piper Tripacers and Cessnas – belonging to the Kenya Police Reserve were employed, flown by the Police.

An Army Air Corps (AAC) helicopter waits to lift a casualty to hospital, Southern Arabia, 1965. (Leo Cooper Collection)

Specially-made-up packs weighing twenty-five pounds each were free-dropped one at a time from the door of the aircraft by RASC air despatchers, the planes making several low runs over the DZ to complete the task.

In Cyprus, too, the political situation between

TOP RIGHT *92 Company East African Army Service Corps (EAASC) On the Nairobi–Nyeri Road, Kenya, during the Mau Mau Emergency, 1955. (Leo Cooper Collection)*

BOTTOM RIGHT *The up-to-date method of air-dropping supplies. An air despatch crew of 47 Squadron (Air Despatch) RCT about to eject pallets from an RAF C130 Hercules aircraft on exercise c1987. (Ministry of Defence – Crown Copyright)*

the British and the Greeks, and the Greeks and the Turks, both had an effect on transport operations on the island. In addition, the British Bases at Akrotiri, Dhekelia and Limassol were for a short time in 1956 involved in the transportation activities connected with the Suez operation, but, since these produce no new types of transportation, will not be considered further. However, in the first of the internal troubles in Cyprus – the campaign against EOKA – which started in April, 1955, there is one transport example deserving of mention. For operations in the Troodos Mountains locally-hired donkeys were employed for some of the infantry units to carry stores and equipment. Although little is recorded of this fact, it is probably the last time that animal transport was used on active operations by a purely British Army Force. At the end of the EOKA troubles, when the United Nations Force – UNFICYP – was established to hold the line between the Greek and Turkish population of the island, a new use of British Army logistic transport was introduced. This involved providing, as a permanent part of UNFICYP, an RCT MT squadron from UK or BAOR, and this is still continued. Squadrons go to UNFICYP on a six-month tour to support the mixed force of British and other nations.

The troubles in Northern Ireland which erupted into a State of Emergency in August, 1969, have produced many problems for the British Army, sent in to help the civil authorities keep the peace. Not the least of these has been to produce better protection for soldiers on vehicle patrol and for the safer troop movement and maintenance of small outposts in areas where opposition to the Army's presence is likely. To meet the first of these requirements two new types of vehicle are now added to those previously considered in the troop-carrying role. These are the Humber 1-ton and the Saracen Armoured Personnel Carrier. These vehicles were initially driven by the infantry units themselves, but in 1972 they became part of the logistic vehicle fleet. They were taken over and are now driven by the

Donkey pack animals in the Troodos Mountains, Cyprus, during operations against Ethniki Organosis Kuprion Agoniston (EOKA) terrorists, 1957. (Leo Cooper Collection)

RCT on all operations in support of the combat arms, and such tasks as bomb disposal, carried out by the RAOC. Both the 1-ton Armoured, known as the Pig, and the Saracen APC were not in their first youth. However, they provided the necessary degree of protection against most attacks, and such attacks they certainly received. These vehicles are still in use in Northern Ireland, but a new improved wheeled APC, the Saxon, is now in production as a general replacement in this range of vehicles.

Although the APCs meet the requirement for safer road movement in unfriendly areas in Northern Ireland, helicopters are now the standard means of transporting both troops and stores over longer distances, to outposts, or for rapid deployment. The jointly produced Anglo-French (Westlands/Aerospatiale) helicopter, the Puma, is the RAF type now generally used. It can carry sixteen fully equipped troops, and in the casualty evacuation role, six stretcher and six sitting cases. It can also carry the equivalent load of stores internally or underslung, but the ageing, but very effective, Wessex is still more commonly used for stores.

In April, 1982, operations were mounted to retake the Falkland Islands, occupied by Argentine forces on 2 April. Completion of the complex logistic preparations necessary to launch such an amphibious operation in the time available was a considerable feat by any standards, only made possible by the technical skills and co-operation of all those involved. No prior plan

TOP LEFT *The Humber wheeled armoured personnel carrier (APC), the Pig, Northern Ireland, c1985. (School of Transportation, RCT – Crown Copyright)*

BOTTOM LEFT *The Saxon armoured personnel carrier, replacement for the Pig and Saracen APCs. (School of Transportation, RCT – Crown Copyright)*

ABOVE *An RAF Puma helicopter lifting Army supplies during an exercise in the United Kingdom, c1982. Ground and air units involved are elements of the British contribution to the NATO Allied Command Europe Mobile Force. (Logistic Support Battalion, ACE Mobile Force, (Land))*

Nurses of Queen Alexandra's Royal Army Nursing Corps embarking on the **Rangatira** *at Southampton for the Falklands Campaign, 19 June, 1982. (Imperial War Museum)*

TOP RIGHT *MV* **Atlantic Conveyor**, *a Ship Taken Up From Trade (STUFT), for the Falklands Campaign, 1982. The ship was later sunk by enemy aircraft and all her stores and Chinook helicopters except one were lost. (Imperial War Museum)*

BOTTOM RIGHT *A Mexeflote of 73 Port Squadron loaded with a mixture of vehicles and stores, Port Stanley, Falklands, 1982. These rafts can lift up to 100 tons. (Headquarters 3 Transport Group RCT)*

for such an operation existed, and with the lines of communication stretching for 8,000 miles from the UK Base, averaging twenty-one days' sailing, the transportation and movements problems were immense. Nevertheless, on 20 May the British Force, commanded by Major-General J. Moore, ultimately of two brigades and supporting troops, landed at San Carlos Bay in the Falklands. To achieve this landing and support the subsequent campaign, it was necessary to transport 9,000 troops, 100,000 tons of stores and ninety-five assorted aircraft, by sea and air, having first assembled both troops and stores at ports and airfields. The vast quantities of stores and ammunition were issued by the RAOC Depots and distributed, under the arrangements of the Movements Staffs by British Rail and RCT supplemented by hired transport, in a remarkably

short time. Marchwood Military Port, with its ability for rapid response to changing requirements and priorities, and its capability for handling a wide range of shipping and cargoes, proved invaluable.

Apart from the Royal Naval Vessels HMS *Hermes* and HMS *Fearless*, which carried the Commando Brigade, the only suitable Service logistic shipping immediately available were four LSLs, and it was necessary to take up from trade over fifty vessels from thirty-three different companies, totalling 673,000 gross registered tons. These included three UK flag cruise liners – *Queen Elizabeth II*, *Canberra* and *Uganda*. The last was fitted out as a hospital ship. In addition to the troopships, there were some well-known ferries and a number of modern container ships. Conversions had to be carried out to some of the vessels, including the fitting of helicopter decks, but all were completed with remarkable speed. The initial Naval Task Force, with 3 Commando Brigade and 2 Parachute Battalion, embarked and sailed from Devonport/Marchwood on 5 April, followed on 9 April by the *Canberra* from Southampton, with additional troops from the Commando Brigade. The liner had been prepared in the remarkably short time of five days. 5 Brigade, and the remainder of the Force, followed in other shipping and by air over the following few weeks.

TOP LEFT *An RAF Chinook helicopter refuelling from rubber air-portable containers, Falklands, 1982. Each container holds 40 gallons and weighs 3757 pounds. (Imperial War Museum)*

BOTTOM LEFT *An RN Sea King helicopter with underslung load passing the burning LSL **Sir Galahad**, Falklands, 1982. (Imperial War Museum)*

BELOW *An AAC Gazelle helicopter picking up a casualty from 1st Battalion, Scots Guards, Tumbledown, Falklands, 1982. (Soldier Magazine)*

A staging base was established at RAF Wideawake on the South Atlantic island of Ascension (ASI), where both troops and stores were flown in by aircraft from the RAF Stations at Lyneham and Brize Norton. Here both were reallocated and transferred to the shipping of the Task Force. The RAF aircraft used were the VC10 passenger aircraft and the C130 Hercules, the principal aircraft for air supply and freight, but now much used in a passenger role. The main logistic helicopter planned for use in the operation was the American Chinook, now in common use in BAOR. This helicopter can carry forty-four fully equipped troops, or a load of 8,164 kgs, which can be carried as an internal or underslung load. Regrettably, all but one of those sent with the Force were lost, when the container ship in which they were stowed, the *Atlantic Conveyor*, was sunk by enemy action in San Carlos Bay. The loss of these aircraft was to make the logistic support of the Force that much more difficult, but initiative, improvisation and technical competence, mingled with blood, sweat and tears, ensured that this setback was overcome.

The LSLs with the Force carried six Mexeflotes between them on their decks. These are normally slung on the sides of the vessels, but, because of the rough seas in the Falklands area, they had to be deck-stowed. These versatile pieces of equipment, formed from interchangeable floating steel cells, can form powered rafts for ferrying, or pontoons, or causeway, and were to be the main means of unloading the vessels of the Force. In the course of the disembarkation of the Force, one of the LSLs – *Sir Galahad* – was set on fire by enemy action with a sad loss of life of soldiers of the Welsh Guards. The vessel was later a total loss.

The Falklands campaign was ultimately won by the great gallantry and military competence of the infantry and the supporting arms on land, the Royal Navy at sea and in the air, and the RAF. It is easy to take for granted, though, the accomplishments of those concerned in turning the most complex logistic plan into the practical, essential, support required to help ensure victory. Much of this support centered round the ability to transport men and material to wherever required. In the Falklands campaign this was successfully achieved, using every agency and nearly every mode of transport.

It is surely right that animals, perhaps now only on grounds of seniority, should occupy a place on the last page of this book. However, the Falklands campaign proved beyond doubt that helicopters have replaced the need for animals in military operations. The training element for animal transport in the British Army, at the RCT Training Centre at Aldershot, was disbanded in 1972 and the last operational unit, 414 Pack Transport Troop RCT, in Hong Kong, in 1976. An era had ended.

The means of transporting the British Army have changed, but the operating of the means still remains a human factor. Whether leading a mule, driving a tank transporter, steering a boat or flying a helicopter, it is the 'Drivers' that make it all possible, and have done over the centuries. It is to them that this book is dedicated.

'Victory is the beautiful bright-coloured flower. Transport is the stem without which it could never have blossomed.' **Winston Spencer Churchill**, *The River War*.

A mule of 414 Pack Transport Troop RCT with fuel for a Royal Air Force Whirlwind helicopter in the New Territories, Hong Kong, c1969. (IRCT)

Bibliography

The following are some of the numerous books to which reference has been made in the preparation of this book, in addition to papers and documents examined in the Libraries and Archives listed in the Acknowledgements:

Troopships and their History Colonel H. C. B. Rogers OBE, Seeley, Service and Co Ltd, Imperial Services Library Vol. VII 1963

The Story of P & O David and Stephen Howarth, Weidenfeld and Nicolson 1986

Hospital Ships and Trains John H. Plumridge OBE, Seeley, Service and Co Ltd 1975

Following the Drum, (Women in Wellington's Wars) Brigadier F. C. G. Page, André Deutsch 1986

The History of the British Army Edited by Brigadier Peter Young and Lieutenant Colonel J. P. Lawford, Arthur Barker Ltd 1970

A History of Warfare Field-Marshal the Viscount Montgomery of Alamein, Collins 1968

The Shorter Pepys Robert Latham, Bell and Hyman Ltd 1985

Mr Pepys' Navy L. A. Wilcox, G. Bell and Sons Ltd 1966

The RASC, A History of Transport and Supply in the British Army, Vol. 1 John Fortescue, Cambridge University Press 1930

The RASC, A History of Transport and Supply in the British Army, Vol. 2 Colonel R. H. Beadon, Cambridge University Press 1931

The Story of the RASC, 1939–1945, The Institution of the Royal Army Service Corps G. Bell and Sons Ltd 1955

The Story of the RASC and RCT edited by Brigadier D. J. Sutton, Leo Cooper, in association with Secker and Warburg 1984

Military Transport Lieutenant Colonel G. A. Furse, HMSO 1882

The British Army Jock Haswell, Thames and Hudson 1985

Britain and her Army Corelli Barnett, Allen Lane 1970

Men of Gallipoli Peter Liddle, Allen Lane 1976

The Turn of the Wheel, (History of the RASC) 1919–1939 Major General P. G. Turpin CB OBE MA, Barracuda Books 1988

Defeat into Victory Field-Marshal Sir William Slim, Cassell 1956

Reminiscences R. E. B. Crompton, Constable 1928

Railways at War John Westwood, Osprey 1980

The Blue Nile Alan Moorehead, Penguin Books 1983

The White Nile Alan Moorehead, Penguin Books 1973

The Seven Ages of the British Army Field-Marshal Lord Carver, Weidenfeld & Nicolson Ltd 1984

Cromwell, our Chief of Men Antonia Fraser, Weidenfeld and Nicolson Ltd 1973

El Alamein to the Sangro Field-Marshal the Viscount Montgomery of Alamein, Hutchinson and Co Ltd

Normandy to the Baltic Field-Marshal The Viscount Montgomery of Alamein, Hutchinson and Co Ltd

This Motoring Stenson Cooke, Automobile Association

The Struggle for Europe Chester Wilmot, Collins 1952

The Development of the English Traction Engine Ronald Clarke, Goose and Son

Record of the Expedition to Abyssinia Holland and Hozier, London 1870

History of the British Army Charles Messenger, W. H. Smith and Son

Index